INDIA A Civilization of Differences

INDIA A Civilization of Differences

The Ancient Tradition of Universal Tolerance

ALAIN DANIÉLOU

Edited and prefaced by Jean-Louis Gabin
Translated from the French by Kenneth Hurry

Inner Traditions
Rochester, Vermont

Inner Traditions
One Park Street
Rochester, Vermont 05767
www.InnerTraditions.com

Originally published in French under the title *La Civilisation des différences* by Kailash Editions

First U.S. edition published in 2005 by Inner Traditions

Calligraphy on page v copyright © 2005 by Hiralal Prajapati

Note: Because classical Sanskrit diacritical marks were handled inconsistently in the original publication of essays included in this collection, the American editor has decided to dispense with them for all U.S. editions of this book. This decision in no way reflects upon Alain Daniélou's personal mastery of Sanskrit.

LIBRARY OF CONGRESS CATALOGING-IN-PUBLICATION DATA
Daniélou, Alain.
    [Civilisation des différences. English]
    India, a civilization of differences : the ancient tradition of universal tolerance / Alain Daniélou ; translated from the French by Kenneth Hurry ; edited and prefaced by Jean-Louis Gabin.
        p. cm.
    Includes bibliographical references and index.
    ISBN 1-59477-048-4
    1. India—Civilization. 2. Caste—India. I. Hurry, Kenneth. II. Gabin, Jean-Louis. III. Title.
    DS423.D17313 2005
    305.5'122'0954—dc22
                                                                    2005007389

Printed and bound in Canada by Webcom Limited

10   9   8   7   6   5   4   3   2   1

Text design and layout by Priscilla Baker
This book was typeset in Sabon, with Bodega Serif and Agenda as the display typefaces

ईश वास्यमिदꣳ सर्वं यत्किंच जगत्यां जगत ।
तेन त्यक्तेन भुञ्जीथा मा गृधः कस्य स्विद्धनम् ॥

ईशावास्योपनिषत् ।

*I — In a world where everything changes [where nothing
is permanent] the divine is everywhere present [in flowers,
birds, animals, in forests, in man].
II — Enjoy fully what the god concedes to you and
never covet what belongs to others [neither their goods,
nor their talent, nor their success].*

ISHA UPANISHAD, TRANSLATED BY ALAIN DANIÉLOU

Contents

Caste and Freedom for Alain Daniélou

Caste problems reared their head in Alain Daniélou's family before his birth. Indeed, his mother belonged to the Clamorgan family, one of the most ancient noble families in Normandy, some of whose members were crusaders. The father of Madeleine Clamorgan was, according to the traditions of his caste, a general in the French Army. She herself was a devout Catholic and devoted to Pius X.[1]

The Daniélou family, on the other hand, was non-religious, with neither glorious family traditions nor noble title. Alain Daniélou's grandfather, the Mayor of Douarnenez, was buried without religious rites, a fact that was scandalous and very rare at that time. Charles, Alain's father, had not been baptized when he met his wife. A member of Parliament, he became the leader of the parliamentary radical party, a movement that was considered to belong to the extreme left. In the thirties, at Châteaulin, a tiny sub-prefecture and Daniélou's constituency, one of my distant relations, Guillaume Laurent—known familiarly as "Tonton Laouïc"—was his electoral agent. They defended secularism and the state schools and violently fought against the clergy and the Catholic movements at a time when the school war was raging in Brittany. They were the "Reds" against the "Whites."

Curiously enough, it was the Dreyfus affair that brought together

Alain Daniélou's parents, persons not very likely to meet. On the subject of this racist affair that divided French opinion, they both declared in the Captain's favor, which may seem evident for Charles, but was much less so for Madeleine, a soldier's daughter.

Very early on, Alain Daniélou became aware of the strange nature of this marriage and the problems it raised. In his memoirs,[2] he writes about his mother: "The truth was that my mother thought of her children as bastards; because she was an uncompromising woman, she must surely have faced that problem at some point in her life. She always refused to introduce us into 'her' world, nor could she bear to see us mingle with her husband's political friends. . . ."

In 1926, Alain Daniélou spent a year at Saint John's College in Annapolis, Maryland. He was amazed at the profound racism he encountered in the United States: the Blacks were relegated outside the towns; he was briskly reprimanded by the college dean for having spent the weekend at the home of a Jewish friend.

In 1930, a study trip to Algeria was cut short because the local colonials looked disapprovingly on this Parisian who frequented the "natives" on an equal footing, the height of dissidence!

His set of articles, *Le Tour du monde en 1936*,[3] gives us a better glimpse of Alain Daniélou's ideas at that time. Speaking about Harlem, where he saw *Macbeth* played by a Negro cast, he wrote: "Shakespeare corrected, arranged, erased by these Negroes, I feel a racial prejudice within me I should never have thought myself capable of. . . . Harlem is boring; I dream of the beauty, the refinement, the poetry of other colored peoples, in the dazzling Indies."

On the American Indians, of whom he was a passionate defender, he wrote: "They contemplate this last defeat: the conquerors, covered with their spoils, ridiculously imitating the dances they danced for the gods. . . . A gust of civilization reaches us like the desert wind when, in the middle of all the pretentious and vulgar junk of imitation products, these objects appear, in which every detail is noble, each line of which has been pondered for centuries."

This first work of his, written in 1936, gives us a foretaste of the orientation of his work, and the great idea that he ceaselessly pursued. "Dazzled" by India, its level of culture and its arts, he devoted his life to obtaining world recognition for the great civilizations of Asia and to showing that Western economic imperialism should not be tied to any kind of cultural imperialism. He never ceased in his struggle to get the West to understand that, for example, the *gagaku*—the orchestra for traditional music at the Japanese court—was comparable to the Berlin Philharmonic, and that the *raga* interpretations of Ravi Shankar are not folklore, but artistic works in no way inferior to those of Mozart, Ravel, or Bernstein. He started with the musical world—to win recognition for the values of an art little known in the West—and then extended his scope to include other sectors.

He decided which side he was on very rapidly and, at Benares, became a "native," violently anticolonial, connected with the orthodox independence movements, to the amazement and reprobation of the occupant British community. He even accepted the designation of *mleccha*, which in Hindi means "a barbarian," one who has not been born on the sacred soil of India. In traditional Indian society, the foreigner, whatever his origin, is classed as a Shudra, that is, as belonging to the artisan and workers' caste, which is by far the most numerous, since it includes about eighty percent of the entire population.

As Alain Daniélou explains in his memoirs, this status—which was his for many long years—is in no way an obstacle to the gaining of knowledge. He was able to study with the *pandits*, the *Brahman* scholars of Benares, so long as he observed the duties of a good Shudra student: vegetarianism, which is not usual for members of this caste; daily ritual bathing in the Ganges; not touching his master; not entering certain parts of his master's house; and so on.

Having become the disciple of the scholarly monk Swami Karpatri, Daniélou spent many years studying traditional cosmology and metaphysics with Pandit Vijayanand Tripathi and the *rudra vina* with Sri Sivendranath Basu. At the order of Swami Karpatri, he was regularly initiated into Hinduism and received the name of Shiva Sharan (the protected, or protégé, of Shiva).

After plunging into the orthodox Hindu world (learning Hindi and Sanskrit and studying philosophy) he became a Hindu himself and returned to Europe to show the West the true face of Hinduism. This orthodoxy—which he made his own—is totally opposed to puritanism, of which his later translation of the *Kama Sutra* is living proof.

He shocked people by his ideas, which separated him from what was in fashion. The Aryan invasions, the barbarian hordes from the north, were for him the end of the golden age of the great civilizations. He opposed the later moralist religions, starting with Buddhism—which he castigated for its proselytism—and in particular the monotheistic religions, Islam and Christianity. Marxism and socialism he considered as pernicious utopias. His Shaivite approach to Hinduism also put him against many Indian circles, which have become, thanks to Western influence, puritan and integralist, contrary to the true spirit of this tradition.

Another problem arose owing to his homosexuality, which he did not hide. He rapidly detached himself from his family and, during his Paris years, led a bohemian life, getting to know Gide, Cocteau, Jean Marais, and even the dancers of the Moulin Rouge: a whole society of suspects that were not very commendable in his family's eyes. From the end of the fifties, he supported Arcadia, one of the first homosexual movements in Europe.

His return from India settled nothing. He did not go unnoticed, since he wore the topknot of the orthodox Hindu.

For a well-known family like his, belonging to the establishment, all this was not without problems. His brother and brother-in-law had just been nominated to the French Academy. Thanks to a joke played by the gods, however, scandal attacked the family in quite another way: the strange death of his brother the Cardinal, under circumstances that compromised his reputation, inspired some of the most beautiful pages in Alain Daniélou's autobiography.[4]

Alain Daniélou's character was given one of its best definitions by Bernard Pivot: "A 'marginal' who has been successful," since throughout his life he evolved in quite different worlds. On the one hand, his austere life with the Indian pandits, with his long and arduous studies of

Sanskrit and music, then the founding and directing of the musicological institutes in Berlin and later in Venice. On the other hand, his life in international society, from Tagore and Nehru to Nicolas Nabokov and Yehudi Menuhin. And lastly, his adventures in the underworld of Pekin, and in the infamous nightclubs of Berlin, where he met Auden, and of Rome, where he frequented the districts made famous by Pasolini.

After the quarrel with his family, a second conflict concerned his society of origin: France, his "tribe," as he used to define it. A religious conflict is also evident. At UNESCO, he spoke English, despite French protests, and represented Hindi writers at a Pen Club meeting. When he settled in Berlin in 1962, he admitted his sympathies for Prussia, and never sought to meet the French, relegated to the far-off "Quartier Napoléon." Finally, he settled in Italy, whose profound paganism he loved.

Unclassifiable, paradoxical, he bestrides the century, touching everything, going everywhere.

Western society is made in such a way that it cannot understand that a character who admits and takes responsibility for his homosexuality, drives a Porsche at 230 km an hour, states in turn that he is a painter or musician, and is equally happy to frequent high society or the common people, can also be a credible scholar, a musicologist, and a philosopher.

Alain Daniélou was also trying to safeguard his freedom of thought and to avoid belonging to any clique or ideology. He wrote:

I have never wanted to belong to any religious sect or belief, never wanted to give up my free will. But, being naturally critical, I have always had a tendency to challenge the dominant ideology, oppose what people take for established truths, always noting that hell is paved with good intentions, and thinking that calling all statements to question is the only way of ensuring that knowledge grows. Debate is part of research, not of assertion. The paradox, the calling to question of what seem to be the soundest proofs, is a salutary exercise, the only one capable of causing progress and not remaining hidebound by dogma. This has often meant that I have been credited with belonging to certain theories that I in no way subscribe to. It is difficult for free minds to find a place in a society infected by equally arbitrary ideological conflicts and parties.

I am not a prophet; even my beard refuses to grow. My age means that people expect me to give them directives or oracles, which I refuse to do. I am not a guru. I still seek to understand the mystery of the world, to which end, every day, I am ready to start all over again, to re-examine my convictions, to reject any belief, to progress only in the direction of knowledge, which is the opposite of faith. I still stolidly mistrust any rite or ceremony, which always appear to me like a piece of theatre when there are witnesses. I refuse to perform a puja for the always fanatical devout (today we would call them "fans"). The only value I never call to question is that of the teachings I have received on Shaivite Hinduism, which rejects all dogmatism, since I have never found any form of thought that goes so far, so clearly, with such profoundness and such intelligence in comprehending the divine and the structures of the world. No form of thought can in any way approach this marvelous quest that comes down to us from the dawn of time. None of the ideologies, none of the theories that divide the modern world seem to me to be worthy of being shared or defended by me. To me, they seem puerile, when they are not merely aberrant.[5]

He not only safeguarded his own freedom of thought, but sought to preserve it for all, as attested by his statement written while this book was being prepared:

According to the Indian theory of cycles, the end of the Age of Conflicts, or *Kali Yuga*, in which we are now living, is marked by standardization, the prelude to death, and by the will to destroy an infinite variety of vegetable, animal, or human species that characterize the beauty of the divine work.

Antiracism, which denies the originality, specificity, and beauty of the different varieties of the human species, has become an intangible doctrine, spreading with a fanaticism that perverts all anthropological, cultural, social, or religious studies.

In India, there has never been any black race of the African type. Most of the population belongs to the brown race. Symbolic colors have been attributed to the different functions that are essential to any society. The fact that black is the color attributed to the working class—which could just as well have been green or pink—immediately rouses hostile reactions, owing to their assimilation to modern conditions in certain countries, expressed with so much violence that a publisher may hesitate to publish a work referring to a civilization that has, for thousands of years, allowed the most different peoples and cultures to coexist without destroying each other.

Such a form of censorship is contrary to the principle of the freedom of expression, carried out in the name of a new dogma, sadly recalling the trials of heretics of the past.[6]

From the time of the publication of his first book in 1936 until 1993, Alain Daniélou wrote—besides about twenty seminal works[7]—several hundred articles and papers for journals, encyclopedias, conferences, radio programs, and so on, some in French, and others in English, Hindi, or Italian.

These texts deal with a very wide variety of subjects concerning India, such as its religion, society, language, yoga, and music. Some have never been published, and most are unobtainable. With the author's agreement, and under his supervision, I began cataloguing these texts according to subject matter, whence the idea of publishing collections of the texts in book form.

Jean-Louis Gabin—who early on took an interest in this project and began working on it while the author was still alive—has undertaken the task of writing the preface, as well as collecting and editing these various texts, which present a previously unpublished viewpoint of Alain Daniélou's work.

JACQUES E. CLOAREC

PREFACE
Sacred Order and Human Society

At the dawn of the twenty-first century, it appears that the Western view of India is starting to change. The reception given to Alain Daniélou's work in Europe and the United States is both one of the signs of this change and one of the causes. Increasingly widely considered as a first rate Indologist, musicologist, and *seeker after truth*, Alain Daniélou is one of the rare Europeans to have been accepted within India's traditional society, for which he became a spokesman. On his return to Europe, he contributed enormously to saving the world's traditional music by setting up the Institute for Comparative Musical Studies in Berlin and Venice. Later he published a series of seminal works on Indian mythology, history, music, sculpture, and social structures that established his international reputation and helped to change the Western view of India.

This book contains unpublished works of Alain Daniélou, as well as papers read at conferences and articles published in journals, which deal with the delicate and controversial theme of the "caste system." These works were all revised, corrected, and expanded by the author toward the end of his life. Occasionally, two similar texts have been combined or cuts have been made where two articles repeated each other, and at times the author redefined his ideas in the light of questions or objections put forward by Jacques Cloarec or myself. As the texts were written over the span of many years—between 1938 and 1991—it is consequently not surprising to find occasional differences of expression and even apparent contradictions, bearing witness to the vital development of his thought.

The articles in this book thus represent various highlights on, or approaches to, a central theme: that of the balance between social cohesion and individual freedom, between the interests of communities and those of the wider entities of which they form part, between human groups and animals, plants, forests, hills, and rivers, traditionally considered in India as manifestations of a sacred order, of which human society is merely a correspondence or reflection.

Such a concept is very far from that of the modern West, which has arisen, first and foremost, out of opposition to the ancient order of things and appears to be entirely centered, not only on the individual and his "rights," but on the economic aspect of his activities. The Western reader must therefore be ready to question his or her habitual judgment, vocabulary, and ideas, and in particular must strive not to politicize[1] the caste question, which has so often been caricatured by modern writers.

The following articles complement the views expressed elsewhere by the author, in particular in his *Virtue, Success, Pleasure, and Liberation; While the Gods Play;* and *Shiva and Dionysus* (reissued as *Gods of Love and Ecstasy*). Daniélou's clarity is there, as well as his sense of being a free man, loving paradox and irony, and belonging—like Marguerite Yourcenar—to a generation that uses, for example, the word "race" without inhibition[2] and without any negative coloring, because in their eyes differences are not only legitimate, but the very basis of harmony and beauty.

Undoubtedly, Alain Daniélou's work and life form a unique bridge between two civilizations, or rather, between two conceptions of the place and role of human societies on our planet. The first, which animates the last still living traditional civilization of the ancient world, has sought to establish a balance, not only between the various human groups, but between these and the natural world, considered as the gods' own country. This is a polytheistic civilization, a civilization of time cycles and mythologies, one that has respect for what is different and one that incorporates the past into the present. The other conception is infinitely more recent, deriving from the linear time of monotheism and the promotion of history by Christianity. It emphasizes a move toward the future, combats differences in the name of equality, rejects tradition in favor of *novelty* and seeks to break nature in the name of culture.

In the nineteenth and twentieth centuries, this modern ideology spread from Europe and North America to "convert" the whole world, with the aid of Christian missionaries, colonizers, socialist and Marxist militants, and liberal reformers.[3] However, at the end of the twentieth century, when its triumph appeared to be total, certain disquieting signs arose to question the certitudes used to sweep away ancient societies and former regimes, often hidebound or corrupt. These signs included the fall of the Berlin wall and the floundering of the Soviet Empire—lighthouse and agent throughout the twentieth century of so many revolutions carried out for the "good" of the people; the return of particularisms, territorial and cultural claims by groups thought to have been "assimilated"; the resurgence of religious life; and resistance to globalization, to a unique philosophy, to the destruction of our ecological balance. These are all signs showing the limits and insufficiencies—and perhaps the mortal danger—sheltered by the ideology that governs our society.

There is no question of denying the successes of the modern world, which at a technological level are remarkable—even if they have also perfected the means of destruction. At a medical level they are astonishing, despite having been achieved at the price of the torture and death of millions of animals used as guinea pigs. Such successes—"information" about which all too often dissimulates the negative side—also serve to disqualify traditional societies, and justify their invasion and destruction.

The outset of the third millennium of what we consider our history hardly bears witness to the triumph of the ideas of happiness and progress that have been used to justify the upheavals in human society over the past three hundred years. Never before have the calamities striking our species and planet been so directly attributable to humanity itself. In our historic memory, nothing approaches such an abundance of massacres, peoples humiliated and parked in camps, civilizations annihilated, vegetable and animal species destroyed.[4] According to Teddy Goldsmith, destruction in the biosphere over the past half-century greatly exceeds everything that humans had previously caused over the span of three million years.[5]

The idea of unlimited material progress ensuring human happiness is no longer seriously defended by anyone. In Third World countries, living conditions have on occasion dramatically worsened as a result of the imposition of industrial agriculture and monocultures, which have exhausted the soil, destroyed social stability, and thrown entire populations into shantytowns. Overpopulation is only the reverse side of a phenomenon that in the West is characterized by a fall in the birth rate: the human animal's response to the various stages of vital precariousness and anguish about the future.

At the same time, the atmosphere in "advanced" countries is hardly reassuring, with the consumption of tranquillizers soaring and psychoanalysis overburdened with patients. One European home out of four consists of a single person, and the number of children raised by single parents is continually on the increase, as well as juvenile distress and delinquency. Senior citizens who not long ago transmitted the oral tradition at the same time as playing an effective role have now been relegated to retirement homes. The crisis in the educational system—now learning how to "sell itself" and giving no place to craftwork, art, or manual and artistic activities—is considerably undervalued, while precarious job tenure is presented as something positive. We seek to forget our condition and the increasingly precise threats that loom over our survival by using medicines, alcohol, drugs, evasion, and strong emotions.

Paul Valéry's well-known dictum that our civilizations now know that they are mortal has for some years become so commonplace that we almost blush to repeat it. Everything happens as though the government of humankind were the plaything of autonomous mechanical fates, "contingencies," "modernism," "economic imperatives," as though political action were restricted to masking the more visibly monstrous aspects of reality. *Maya*, the power of illusion, is undoubtedly the most pervasive phenomenon in this industrial society, at the same time so proselytizing and so lacking in gods.

Behind the wave of information bearing emotions, self-satisfaction, cupidity—and almost never intelligence—what framework is there for us to think not only of the threatened future of the world and the generations to come, but of our own immediate future? The ideologies that astounded us until recently have, one after the other, come to be seen as ethnocentric, predatory systems, responsible for the destruction of traditional civilizations, for persecuting independent thinkers, for the dichotomy of body and spirit, for the mortal divorce between humans and nature.

The Mexican Dream by Jean-Marie Gustave Le Clézio gives a perfect illustration of the Church's role of providing spiritual justification for the genocide of the Amerindian peoples, the prelude to and condition for the founding of the modern era on that continent.[6] Moreover, we all too often forget that colonial ideology, even between the two world wars, enjoyed political consensus, as evidenced by Léon Blum's statement to the French Parliament on July 9, 1925, which would be flabbergasting today: "We admit the right, and even the duty, of the superior races to draw to themselves those who have not achieved the same degree of culture and to call them toward progress, realized through the efforts of science and industry."[7]

Is Alain Daniélou entirely wrong in noting, in an article on cultural genocide included in this book that, "Although colonialism has nowadays abandoned—in Africa as in other 'third-world' countries—its most brutal forms of genocide and slavery, the concepts of cultural and racial superiority it used as its justification have not been sincerely revised"? Questioning of these concepts only really began, in the United States and in Europe, at the end of the sixties, with emerging demands of respect for traditional cultures and civilizations and a renewal of the teaching of regional languages, which the period that followed the French Revolution, called the Terror, and later the Third French Republic, had systematically fought. This view was bolstered by the emergence of the ecology movement and the idea of the "Right to be Different," claimed by antiracist organizations and sexual minorities.[8]

But the idea dawning now, at the outset of the twenty-first century, is not merely a widening awareness of the limitations and predatory nature of "modernism." At a historical and philosophical level, these had already been exposed by Alexis de Tocqueville, or Hippolyte Taine in his *Origins of Contemporary France,*[9] and later on, by François Furet.[10] In the metaphysical field too, the work of René Guénon, of which one title—*The Crisis of the Modern World*—is emblematic, made it possible to analyze, as early as the twenties, the *nature* of the anti-traditional direction taken by the West.[11]

The new idea that appears to the contemporary mind is that the exactions that accompanied the conquests of modern ideology can no longer be considered as necessary evils, passing ills, the sequels of a past that is best forgotten so as not to impede the "globally positive" march toward a "radiant future." Nowadays, it is far clearer that the Terror of 1793, the Gestapo and the death camps,[12] the Gulag archipelago, the Chinese Cultural Revolution, the horrors and persecutions that continue to unfold all around us, are not incidental phenomena, unconnected with each other, but plunge their roots in the totalitarianism of the Holy Inquisition or of Calvin, and even in Rousseau's highly dogmatic *Social Contract.*[13]

In a word, they are the outcome of the "clean sweep" and the radical systems dreamt up by some "genius" or other who, equipped with his rationalism, never doubts his own "common sense" and good intentions, his capacity to remake the world, which "post-modernism" is beginning to question seriously. The catastrophes and threats only partially hidden by the ever-accelerating onward rush of modern humankind invite reflection, if there is still time. They also invite us really to examine—this time without pre-conditions nor preconceived ideas—whether the ways of being and living that preceded the modern world or which have managed to survive side-by-side with it (and often against it) contained something that could be useful for the future of humankind and of the planet, something from which the people of today may draw some inspiration, wisdom, or experiences that could be to our advantage.

There is no doubt that this explains the West's growing interest in India, the only country in which—despite wars, invasions, colonial aggression, and the sometimes brutal irruption of modernism—a multicultural, multiethnic and multireligious traditional society has kept alive a remarkable tolerance and remarkable solidity for thousands of years, as Alain Daniélou has shown.[14]

India, which until the eighteenth century almost alone evoked Europe's "East"—the origin and goal of so much admiration and so many dreams—was described by travelers as a brilliant civilization possessing fabulous riches, religions that recalled those of the ancient world, and a highly structured social system similar to the corporations of Europe in the Middle Ages, which the Portuguese named the caste system. In his *Genius of India*—whose title reveals the new perception of that country—Guy Sorman rightly emphasizes the fact that Western observers' opinion of the caste system was for a long time not particularly reproving.[15] Writers like Nicholas-Jacques Desvaulx, in his book *Moeurs et Coutumes des Indiens*, which was published in Paris in 1777, recognized that the overlapping of the "corporations" (or "communities" as Guy Deleury prefers to call them) gave Indian society a remarkable solidity and made excessive tyranny avoidable.[16] This peculiarity of Indian society, whose diversity was in some way constitutional, was underlined by eighteenth-century philosophers such as Voltaire and Diderot in their fight against intolerance—monotheistic intolerance in particular.

During the nineteenth and twentieth centuries, the European view of India changed entirely, in line with the West's role as "Messiah of a new order," the result of the English and French middleclass revolutions, which would culminate in the systematically antitraditionalist spirit we know today. Starting from 1789, the myths of "civilization" and "progress" invaded the world. The new ideas brought "liberty" and "equality" to all humankind, whether by force as in the

Napoleonic wars, or by means of colonial adventures. Upon contact with the West, entire civilizations, traditions, languages, and populations disappeared beneath what the Marxists coldly termed the "wheel of History." In the eyes of all "progressive" politics, whether Marxist or Christian, India became the very symbol of a "reactionary" society,[17] preferring the solidity of social systems inherited from the past to the egalitarian concepts of the modern world.

Now that it is possible to begin assessing the political and social utopias of the twentieth century,[18] humankind, according to certain people, is faced with a reckoning of accounts and continual crisis management: the former colonizers find it difficult to welcome the former colonized on their own soil; the chorus praising urban civilization is becoming aware that the cities can no longer continue serenely to absorb the rural populations; the preachers of "increase and multiply" are beginning to perceive that the planet cannot be extended, and that if we continue to destroy forests and animal and vegetable species on an industrial scale, modern humanity will become its own species' worst enemy; the "nation-state" so dear to the bourgeois revolutions is under threat owing to the vast extent of ecological problems that can only be dealt with by supranational structures; lastly, the cult of the individual is starting to find its limits, and although a great deal is still said about the "rights of man," people are seriously beginning to ask questions about his *duties*,[19] and are consequently taking a new look at traditional notions such as *dharma*, whose link with the caste system is essential, as will be seen in the following articles.

The challenges of the twenty-first century are everywhere before us: pollution, overpopulation, intolerance, fanaticism, the results of a "science without a conscience," and a materialistic civilization, all of which have profoundly transformed and disenchanted the world. The objective study of a system that has allowed civilization to continue to the present day without genocides or major persecutions may be for us a matter of survival. If it proves correct that, under such a system, differences coexist and collaborate instead of exchanging mutual threats; if this system generates a direct democracy controlled by federations of groups on a human scale (the *panchayats*); if this kind of self-government, or self-control, makes it possible to contain the all-too-easily inhuman and despotic tutelage of the state or of industrial lobbies within certain limits, then the multicultural societies arising with the dawn of postmodernism will need to study it.

This does not mean to say that the caste system has no defects, having been fought against by the early Buddhists, the colonizers, Christian missionaries, and Marxists, or even that it is a panacea, as so many Western systems have claimed themselves to be. Still less does this mean preaching an inverse revolution for the West. It simply means attempting to better understand a prestigious and still living civilization, and not judging it on the basis of clichés, asking ourselves whether we can draw some conclusion from our analysis and whether we have the right to discredit it systematically in our books, films, newspaper articles, and other media.

Indeed, many of the events announced or unfolding around us would require from us an effort of reflection at least equal to the unprecedented means of destruction that the modern world has developed. Are we capable of it? Is it not true that the most powerful information medias' first and foremost aim is "distraction," in Pascal's meaning of the term? And, as for our intellectual elites, do they have any framework for expressing, in full independence, any real freedom of thought, or are they the prisoners of pressure groups bent on ensuring that their own immediate interests come before any search for the truth? Are we already in the situation described by the *Laws of Manu* and the *Vishnu Purana*, in the end of the Kali Yuga, when—the balance among the four castes having been broken and the family destroyed—a declining humanity lives through a succession of partial and myopic dictatorships, that of the priests, of the military, of the traders, and lastly of the workers?

It is somewhat disquieting to learn that, since India's independence and the adoption of a constitution copying Western concepts, "no work on the castes in India has been published that does not start with the rejection of the principle of *Homo Hierarchicus*,"[20] and that, since Louis Dumont's seminal work on the topic,[21] Indian specialists have been careful not "to ask such wide questions on the castes generally; a certain academic prudence [requiring] that the system be condemned en bloc,"[22] even though Dumont has shown that the system seems to be founded on "values shared" by the Indians, not on "necessity," and that the "distribution of functions necessarily leads to exchanges."[23]

Could we but hear today Alain Daniélou's dissenting voice, independent and serene, conveying that basic proposition of Hindu philosophy, "In all things, leveling is death," or hear him say, "The kind of racism that justifies conquest, slavery, the elimination of peoples, and a certain kind of antiracism that promotes assimilation, denies differences, are in fact two forms of imperialism." "The spread of literacy, identified with culture, has been a factor in destroying civilizations belonging to the oral tradition, which have preserved a heritage thousands of years old." "At the level of human society, male and female duties are fundamentally, irremediably, opposed, and it is only when they follow opposite and complementary rules that these two halves of humankind can be fully realized and equal."

This book attempts to show the variety of approach, the breadth of the investigation, and the paradoxical, stimulating, and multifaceted questioning of Alain Daniélou. This is why it groups together a series of articles tackling from various points of view the question of caste, to which the author has devoted a fundamental work,[24] but which remains particularly subject to distortion.

Three leading articles deal with it directly, the third with regard to what the West terms antiracism, a term which, according to Daniélou, most of the time hides—beneath a sometimes sincere sentimentalism— a morbid fear of differences, a strong desire to level everything, very close to the racism it claims to oppose. Here a spate of questions would necessitate a real debate of ideas, separate from the electoral considerations that all too often pervert discourse in our society. Perhaps, after the riots of the past few years in the United States and the violence in European suburbs, we should ask whether the will to assimilate foreign communities, in the physiological meaning of the term, is not itself the source of the general disintegration, despair, and hate, the details of which teachers in public schools on the outskirts and in certain districts of our cities could draw up in an appalling list.

An illustration of the caste system is included with the description of the Ahirs of Benares. Viewing their costumes, their poetry, and dances, which have not been degraded to folklore, we may feel nostalgia at the idea of what the Bretons, the Basques, and the *langue d'Oc* peoples could have transmitted to us. The Ahirs' erotic dances recall certain popular cults condemned by the church, as well as the rites that still exist today among the Sufis, the Aissaouas, and the Berber peoples of North Africa, related to polytheism, to phallic and Dionysian cults. They remind us that the civilizations from which we draw our roots neither prohibited sex nor were guilty of violent attacks on nature, which they did not consider as something inert.

The article on "The Hindu Woman and the Goddess," as well, cannot help but raise questions. Although we may be too close to judge all the effects of the "emancipation" of women in industrial society, its consequences on female solitude and the mental balance of children raised in kindergartens by mercenary assistants are clear. Here, too, it seems that we have desperately sought first and foremost to deny any differences, to unite social roles to the extent of making it difficult to reproduce life in a stable environment providing security. The mirage of the marriage of love, of passion as the basis for social organization, can only be explained by the confusion of individual and social ethics, which the Hindus so wisely distinguish. But the coverage given to this mirage by the media is also a consequence of the puritanism inherited by our society.[25] The religious authorities, whose reign preceded the media's own, did their utmost to channel eroticism exclusively through the institution of marriage, which is nowadays crumbling with the rest of the social fabric.

Pursuing this discussion would take us too far. It is better to allow the reader to discover the article on the dictatorship of the scribes and the underside of *alpha-bêtise*, the one devoted to cultural genocide in Africa, the blasting analysis of the work of Abbé Dubois, the response to the biologist Jacques Ruffié, the article on rights and duties . . . which together provide abundant material for reflection, for questioning and comparison, for those who seek.

JEAN-LOUIS GABIN

The Caste Institution

Certain significant developments in modern science have been the result of interdisciplinary research on the nature of the real, coupled with a rejection of the theological concepts of the Hebrew prophets or of medieval scholasticism.

Modern astrophysicists, atomic physicists, and psychologists have been astonished to discover, in the most ancient concepts of Indian thought, a methodological model and intuition of the nature of the world that go in the same direction as their own ideas, sometimes even surpassing their most audacious speculations.

In Indian philosophy, the two allied methods of *samkhya* and *yoga*—the parallel studies of the structure of the world and the nature of humankind—have made it possible to produce a universal theory on the energetic origin of matter, the omnipresence of consciousness, the nature of individuality, the role of species, and an admirable logic that comprises all aspects of knowledge and life.

Thanks to remarkable genetic data and knowledge of the elaborate selection processes that determine individual aptitudes and mental capacities, a social system has been established in India to correspond to human nature and allow races to coexist in a wittingly diversified society. It reflects the understanding that—before functioning as an individual—every living being claims group membership. Each of us claims to be French or German, Catholic or Protestant, Sikh or Hindu, Muslim or Buddhist.

1

The Hindu social system is a truly noteworthy effort to establish a society that is coherent and harmonious, utilizing and allowing the coexistence of highly different ethnic groups, races, ways of life, and belief. This system—which has permitted Indian civilization to attain an unrivalled continuity—has had to face difficult conditions for more than six centuries. The Muslim invasions, then British colonization and the socializing democracy of modern India have all sought to destroy its foundations. They have not managed to do so, but they have paralyzed its normal development and blocked its evolution and adaptation to the modern world. The caste system is certainly not perfect, but the abuses to which it can give rise have often been exaggerated and stigmatized by the occupying powers, who welcomed any argument that could be used to denigrate traditional society values.

Despite the efforts of the British Government, Muslim egalitarianism, and the social laws of independent India, nothing has seriously broached the Hindu social system, which continues to govern life for most of India's inhabitants. The real people of India comprise innumerable artisan castes, the Shudras, who constitute the vast majority of the population. They are surrounded by an executive triangle of priest-scholars, warrior-princes, and middleclass tradesmen.

All societies are based on some similar division. The French society into which I was born was split into very clear-cut groups. You were a Breton or a Norman, an Alsatian or from Provence. The most marked differences were religious ones: Catholics, Protestants, Jews. As children, we used to run quickly past the Protestant church at Neuilly, where mysterious and diabolical rites were held. We used to hear talk about the terrible problems involved in marriages between Catholics and Protestants, because one no longer knew to which group the children belonged.

The good Breton girls who looked after us were all of peasant stock. They came to work for respectable right thinking middleclass families in Paris in order to acquire a certain polish and good manners. Then they went back to the country to marry a young man from their own circle. When we were invited to their weddings, we were surprised to learn that their dowry, which included farms, herds of cattle, land, masses of linen, and superb gold-embroidered velvet costumes, was probably a hundred times more than my sisters could ever hope for. Yet they treated us respectfully, as persons belonging to a superior social class. There were also the Spaniards who sold fruit, and other foreigners whom one didn't trust. All these people lived side by side, without any problems, but without any familiarity.

When I settled on the banks of the Ganges, in the highly orthodox society of Benares, I never remarked any great difference between social relations there and those I had known in France. Each person was proud to belong to a caste that constituted a sort of extended family. There were, of course, the Brahmans, but also the Banias, or tradesmen; there were princes, as well as Nepalese soldiers; there were Ahirs, who raised cows and claimed Krishna for their own; there were the boatmen, musicians, Sikhs, Muslims, the Doms, who cremated the dead, together with innumerable other groups. I never noticed any jealousy or envy among the various groups, the more so since wealth had nothing to do with their relationships. There were very poor Brahmans, very rich Doms, millionaire Banias, and wretched Kshatriyas.

For each person, the caste, the extended family, was the center of interest. To be elected to the committee of five, the panchayat, which settled disputes within the caste, was a coveted honor. My cook was an outcaste Kshatriya: his mother, born into a great princely family, had been seduced by a Nepalese soldier. Thus he was an outcaste. On the contrary, my boatman, a magnificent young man who was very fond of sport, was a member of the panchayat of his caste. He also took part in wrestling tournaments organized by the Mahant, the high priest of the temple of Kali, who was himself an excellent wrestler. Perhaps because all the participants were rubbed with oil, these men, who never touched each other in their daily lives, seemed to find nothing disturbing in their hand-to-hand contests.

One of the great scholars of the area expounded texts from the *Ramayana* and the *Upanishads* every day in public from the courtyard in front of his house. His very numerous audience included people from all castes, arranged according to rank in small groups. I frequently visited this great scholar to ask questions about traditional mythology and philosophy. Since I was low-caste (foreigners being mlecchas, hence untouchables), I could only sit on the ground in a room outside his house and had to be careful not to touch anything. In return for a minimum of conventions, our relations were very cordial.

The arrangement of Hindu social structures and the related impermeability of ethnic groups has given Hindu society a remarkable stability and allows each category to associate with similar groups without causing them to lose their individuality. This is the case of the Maratha Brahmans of Scythian origin, or the Jats and Sikhs associated with the warrior-princes, or the Parsis of Iranian origin, incorporated among the merchant castes.

It is the symbolic hierarchy of the *varnas*—the four groups identified by the law-giver Manu—which has distorted foreigners' view of the real structures of the system, to the point that they end up believing that most Indians, besides the executives, are a formless mass of dispossessed wretches, or even untouchables, whereas in reality there are a great number of groups, highly independent, taking a great pride in themselves, whose cultural and social heritage is, besides the Aryan contribution, the very basis of Indian civilization.

It is through a characteristic aberration of modern ideology that, under the pretext of abolishing executive prerogatives, popular culture has been ignored and a great effort has been made to destroy privileges, to disorganize institutions, and suppress the Shudras' means of defense, meaning that of the Indian people as a whole.

Among the traditional circles in which I was living, no one understood what Mahatma Gandhi wanted with his propaganda in favor of the so-called untouchables and against the caste system. Everyone is untouchable, particularly the Brahmans, and it seemed as though all the artisan castes (ninety percent of the population) had been mistaken for the families of cesspool clearers who, in every society, had always been kept aside for hygienic reasons. It was not the Brahmans who demonstrated against the official abolition of castes, but all the general population whose identity was going to be lost. My boatman, Ram

Prasad—although his caste is very close to the untouchables since boat-men transport the dead—supported Rashitriya Svayam Sevak Sangh, the ultra-conservative party, and was imprisoned for some time by the Nehru government, together with respectable Brahmans and the famous Sannyasi whose works I had translated.

The great musician who had been my teacher belonged to a family of *zamindars* (landowners), some kind of provincial squires. He never played in public, which would have meant a loss of standing and, above all, stealing the livelihood of traditional musicians. Furthermore, it was in defense of this principle that I recently criticized one of the princesses of Monaco, who uses her position to take up the job of a popular singer. I remember that, in my boyhood, when a famous musician sug-gested that I might have a career as a pianist, my mother was quite indignant: "My son! On the stage! That's unheard of!"

It would appear that the rich middleclass Indians raised in England—like Gandhi and Nehru—never really got to know the general population of India. They were strongly affected by certain social problems, the extent of which the British had been happy to exaggerate, without real-izing what the advantages of the traditional social system were and how much all the ethnic groups were attached to their traditions and their autonomy. Modern egalitarianism does not stop the French from consid-ering themselves first and foremost as Bretons or Basques, Catholics or Jews. The attempt to abolish the caste system in India created many more problems than it solved. The caste is a family, and human beings always need to belong to a group. The abolition of caste in Europe led logically to the destruction of the family, to the terrible isolation of the individual, and to the creation of social protection systems as a substitute.

If we examine the world, the work of the creator, what surprises us most is probably its infinite variety, the perfection and beauty of the dif-ferent forms of life—insects, animals, plants, and humans—and the bal-ance that makes them coexist and be mutually dependent. An animal never kills living beings other than those that are part of its diet, or sometimes, among its own species, those that encroach on its territory, its *lebensraum* or living space.

Like other species, human beings include a great number of varieties, races, colors, aptitudes, and ethics, but also cultures, languages, beliefs, and religions. The fundamental notion of freedom implies a respect for these differences. No species is in itself better or superior to any other. In what way are elephants superior to ants? As individuals, they are not comparable. It is at this point that certain simplistic ideas about the equality of human beings become absurd and pernicious, allowing the strong, the crafty, or the fanatic to crush or dispossess the weak and moderate. All social theories that claim to ignore differences between races and human groups in defining their rights lead to the crushing of the weak, to genocide, and imperialism. This occurs on many levels, since the force of aggression is not based solely on physical strength. It can be technical, linguistic, or religious, just as well as racial.

The Pygmies, who formerly populated Europe and Africa, were gradually dispossessed first by the Mediterranean peoples, then by Indo-Europeans, then by black Africans. Only a few rare tribes now survive, having taken refuge in the forests of southeast Africa. Traditional India, on the other hand, has always recognized the primitive tribes' right to survive with their own way of life. This is not entirely the case nowadays, when they are considered to be backward groups of the population.

Recognition and respect for the various communities and varieties of the human species is a basic principle, used as the foundation stone in the organization of Hindu society, and has made India a refuge for all persecuted peoples, elsewhere threatened with extinction or assimilation.

The caste institution is an application, on a social level, of a general conception of the nature of the world and of living beings. It is certainly not without faults, but is still a model showing how the most different human groups can coexist.

We have much to learn from an institution which, for thousands of years, has made it possible for the most different peoples to live together without tearing each other to pieces, meaning that Indian civilization is practically the only one that has been able to survive culture shocks and maintain its continuity since prehistory.

Hinduism and Human Behavior

Hinduism is not a dogmatic religion. It is not even a religion in the Judeo-Christian sense of the word. What binds Hindus together is a common search, the utilization of all perceptive, intuitive, and intellectual means in the attempt to pierce the enigma of the visible and invisible world. It is an effort to comprehend our deepest nature and our role in the cosmic order, so that we can best fulfill that role collectively and individually. Thus, human beings take an active part in the work of creation, accelerating their own development by collaborating with the gods. This bond of common discovery that unites all Hindus resembles more closely the bond that exists between scientists in the modern world, rather than the somewhat artificial divisions of hereditary beliefs that divide religions.

The opposite of knowledge is belief, the Hindu scholar explains. You believe in something because you do not know it. Dogma, by its very nature, is an assertion of ignorance. Our human objective is to know, to use all the means at our disposal—even those that are most intuitive—to feel and then understand the nature of the world and its transcendent aspects, which we call the divine, without ever erecting the barrier of over-precise definition, of dogma that shuts the door to deeper perception or more abstract concepts. Thus any definition of the tangible world of the cosmos or of the supernatural must necessarily take the form of a hypothesis, valid only up to a certain point. The texts summarizing the metaphysical conceptions of the ancient Hindus are called the "Approaches," the *Upanishads*. Even when their definitions are envisaged as revelations, they cannot assume the role of absolute truths because they are transmitted by means of language, that is, through a code of symbols that belongs essentially to the field of the relative.

Such an intellectual stance leads to a moral and social conception that is very different from that of other religions. For Hindus, ethics is not something negative, like observing taboos, since nothing is forbidden, except on a purely conventional and utilitarian social level, such as police regulations forbidding theft or murder in peace time, whereas they are encouraged in times of war. This is because killing or stealing has, in actual fact, nothing to do with our spiritual development. For Hindus, true ethics are something positive, the practice of certain physical and intellectual disciplines with the aim of perfecting our body and the mental faculties that are inseparable from it. The body is the instrument, the basis of all our spiritual realizations. Hence that training, at once sporting, psychological, and psychical, represented by the initial stages of Hatha Yoga, which aims at perfecting, refining, and developing our means of perception in the tangible and supersensible order.

Every person has a double function. As individuals, we must accomplish our own spiritual destiny while, as members of a social group, we possess a collective destiny: we must ensure the continuity of the species and collaborate in creating a favorable framework for human life. For each person, there are consequently two sets of ethics that often contradict each other, oppose each other, and between which we must, on occasion, choose. This is why a person who wishes to devote himself entirely to his inner development has to relinquish any participation in the social order and must lead the independent life of the wandering sage. We must remember that such a life does not necessarily imply asceticism, nor even compliance with the most elementary laws of the social order.

The word *dharma,* which is often translated as "religion," means "compliance with its nature." Religious teaching can merely advise the individual to realize his or her nature, to seek to perfect it. For each of us, the basic question is to determine what we *are,* individually and socially, and then to define a line of conduct that can help us perfect ourselves. No two individuals are identical. Each of us is the culmination of a different heredity, of different conditions in former lives. We have highly different aptitudes, instincts, tendencies, and capacities. It is consequently quite impossible to define a common set of ethics, or line of conduct for all people, or even for two individuals. We can, however, establish certain scales of values, a certain hierarchy that can serve as a general standard, so long as we know that they are highly relative generalizations and subject to exceptions.

Social ethics are based on the individual's functional role in the complex mechanism of a developed civilization that constitutes a framework through which certain aspects of the nature of the tangible world can be studied at greater depth. In an organized society, social ethics vary according to function, in order to maximize the individual's effectiveness in the social context. This is what caste ethics are. A caste is not a hierarchy with some who are privileged and others who are despised. It must not be forgotten that the notion of transmigration— at all events some form of previous life and the survival of the subtle being—means that today's prince may be reborn as a woodcutter, and the proud Brahman an impure shoemaker.

The conscious being, the inner luminous being, is equal and worthy of respect in all persons alike. But, in just the same way that the law which governs the world—as if it were a law of chance—means that one person is born handsome, vigorous, intelligent, and another deformed and stupid, it also means that one is born a prince and the other a worker. It is up to us to achieve perfection in the state in which we are born, since to a certain extent, that state also forms part of our nature. No social status, no kind of profession, is in itself any more worthy of respect, or any more necessary, than another. Although it is true that the professions of priest or prince entitle a person to certain honors or privileges, it is at the price of rigid duties that make such professions little envied by those belonging to other castes.

For the Hindus, any society involves functional divisions into scholars, warriors, tradesmen, and workers. If any attempt is made to suppress these divisions, they reappear almost immediately under different forms, because they are one of the characteristics of society. Recruitment could be envisaged in ways other than by birth, which would, however, involve more inconveniences and injustices than advantages, since it is simply the family's livelihood and does not affect the intellectual or inner life, which remains outside social divisions. It should not be forgotten that many great poets, artists, and some of India's most venerated mystics have been what we call, without understanding anything thereby, untouchables. Indeed, only the Brahmans are really untouchables owing to their ritual and sacred functions.

Since the division of society on a functional basis corresponds to the nature of the human species, the individual must—except in very rare cases—comply with the position in the hierarchy that his birth assigns to him. It is no worse to be born a soldier, tradesman, or carpenter than it is to be born an oak, elm, tiger, or rabbit. This is the Indian doctrine of the equivalences of social advantages, which is realistic and practical, unlike equality, which is illusory. It is only by recognizing first and foremost the social nature of human beings and by regulating the rights and duties of each functional group that we shall be able to reduce injustices and prevent abuses. It is irrational to attempt to assign the same rights and duties to men and women, to scholars and soldiers, because this never corresponds to reality and prevents each group from being given the different privileges it needs and to which it is entitled.

Each group has different duties, and consequently different virtues. The dharma of a prince is a knightly code of honor, justice, and protection of the weak. The dharma of a prostitute is to practice her trade well and to enrich it by practicing the arts. Each group has different ethical rules established with a view to facilitating its professional effectiveness, and developing the peculiar qualities its members need. Scholars and tradesmen are vegetarians, while warriors and workers are meat-eaters. Rules of marriage are different with regard to the degree of consanguinity allowed, which leads to the development of very different human types. Divorce, which is forbidden for Brahmans, can be easily obtained by workers. A Brahman may take a second wife if his first wife is barren, but a prince is entitled to a vast polygamy.

A man's unfaithfulness is of no consequence to himself, his family, race, and caste, whereas a woman's has to be severely circumscribed, since it affects heredity and the family. The Hindus consider the erotic sphere one of the main arts, but it is practiced with women other than one's chief wife, whose family function is sacred. Sexual fantasies can thus be played out particularly with dancer-prostitutes, formerly attached to the temples, who are greatly honored owing to the essential role they play in protecting society and the family by channeling men's erotic surplus.

Homosexuality is recognized as a biological fact, given the necessity for all the intermediate degrees between masculine and feminine, and has never been persecuted. Its various practices are described in the classical treatises on the art of love, which every young scholar must study in just the same way as the other traditional sciences. Even today, boy prostitutes have their niche in society and certain privileges, in particular, that of playing female roles—dressed as women—at major religious performances, organized by the temples in each town or village, and representing episodes of the epics that recount the lives of the divine heroes Rama and Krishna.

Each caste has its own justice system, administered by a council of notables, and its own laws on inheritance, marriage, divorce, and the sharing out of family assets. It has its own festivals, rites, gods, and costumes, forming a separate and contented world that collaborates harmoniously with the other castes, but never mixes with them. Hence there are two taboos: that of sharing a meal with another caste—which is easily explained since dietary restrictions differ from one caste to another—and that of marrying between different castes. For the man, therefore, an amorous adventure has no consequences and no risks, save those that he may cause the woman to run if she is not a prostitute. But marriage outside the caste is an unpardonable fault, since marriage is the basic social institution, its sole scope that of establishing a home in which children can grow up and develop. The idea of marriage conceived as a ritual act sanctioning sexual relations between two persons who—belonging neither to the same race, nor society, nor to the same religion—can consequently never constitute a link in the chain transmitting certain family and social virtues, appears to Hindus as a joke that is as sacrilegious as it is useless.

Love, a temporary and unreasonable passion, cannot serve as the basis of the social contract that is marriage. Not that the value of love is unappreciated but, like monastic detachment, it is deemed to have an antisocial and purely individual value. Indeed, according to the poets, divine love can only be compared to an adulterous, unreasonable, disinterested, absolute love that is destructive of human values, whereas legitimate love is interested, material, conventional, and binds one to the world. Passion can lead a human being to divine love, but not to the virtue of marriage. Here, individual ethics contradict social ethics.

A person must analyze himself, recognize his physical and mental handicaps, and establish the rules of conduct that help him to overcome those aspects of his individual nature that hinder his spiritual development. Whatever in his conduct helps to free him is good. Whatever tends to bind him to his social status is bad. The same action may thus be good for one and bad for another, according to their nature, just as it can be blameworthy on the social level yet praiseworthy on the individual level.

No rule can be established. The puritan's aggressive external virtue with its repercussions of social honorability can be a greater obstacle than vice or crime at the level of spiritual development. Each of us must choose how far we can go in the ethical nonconformity that frees us from our human ties, without infringing social order—which is also necessary—but which in return risks depriving us of the freedom we are seeking in order to perfect our physical, mental, and spiritual nature.

The notion of nationalism has no place in a hierarchical society. In India it is a foreign import and is only found among recently formed political circles with their entirely non-Hindu ideology. There are, of course, various linguistic and racial groups in India. But only the primitive tribes, which Hinduism has never managed to assimilate, behave like "nations." The states are the spheres of princely administration, whereas social divisions take no account of state borders. People marry within their caste from one end of India to the other; corporative solidarity is complete and ignores artificial political barriers.

This can be found wherever the notion of caste reappears: among proletarian groups, the nobility, the Jews, even in the sectors of high finance and industry, which tend to ignore national frontiers. In actual fact, recognition of the nature of racial and professional divisions, of the caste as the natural basis of society, is probably the only remedy for the excesses of nationalism—and total war which is its logical outcome—since it allows each ethnic group, as well as every social group, to cooperate without the risk of losing their individuality.

It is often said that the hierarchical corporative division of society hinders the progress of modern technical development. Such an assertion appears to be mistaken. Indian experience demonstrates that the princely states, which did not seek to alter traditional society, were modernized much more easily and efficiently than British India and than today's national India, where technical and industrial development have been tied to the adoption of social, ethical, and religious concepts inspired by the West. With its wealth of cultural, social, administrative, and religious values, with its festivals, rites of work, its notables, and its own internal courts, the corporation is a more solid and more effective basis for modern society, in which specialization is mandatory, than the vague collective organisms that defend only the interests of otherwise badly defined social groupings. The corporation can, with efficiency, take on responsibilities in a social order in which it holds an honored position. At this point,[1] we shall not deal with the so-called "untouchables," or Pariahs, which are mostly groupings of persons who have placed themselves outside their caste for offenses judged to be against the social order. Such groups have been exploited by colonial and missionary propaganda to justify their attacks on Hindu civilization.

According to Indian philosophy, there are four aims in human life, which must all be attained. These aims are material achievement (success and fortune), physical well being (sexual pleasure and flowering), virtue (self-realization as a social and ethical being), and liberation, which means abandoning all these achievements to attain union with the divine. These four aims are interdependent. It is almost impossible to achieve one of them without the others. The fullness of happiness and human success is the best basis for renunciation. The spiritual kingdom is not a refuge for the frustrated, for failures, for the weak, nor for those who, through their ambition, wish to be other than they are.

The human being's final goal is spiritual development. Having accomplished his duty as a man, having paid his debts to his parents, his teachers, and society, a man must seek identification of his individual being with the universal being. A man pays his debt to his parents by begetting children, to his teachers by teaching, toward society by accomplishing his social role. Then, finally, he can devote his attention to himself, to that inner, divine being dwelling within his physical and subtle body.

On leaving childhood behind, man's normal life is thus divided into four stages whose relative duration may vary greatly. First comes the life of the celibate student, followed by the existence of the married man, dedicated to material life, pleasure, the founding of a family, and the education of his children. A man must then abandon his material goods and retire with his wife to a peaceful place where he can devote himself to reflection and study. After this, he must abandon his retreat in order to practice the solitary deprivation of the beggar monk, renouncing all social virtues so as to devote himself entirely to his own spiritual liberation.

Such a conception of the world, ethics, and religion is what most Hindus believe in today. Clearly, it is under attack by India's current political leaders, the typical tools of the second step in Western colonialism, which grants peoples administrative and political independence—often more apparent than real—so long as they behave according to the moral standards or social concepts of the West. This means that their physical freedom is sold to them in exchange for the loss of their social and ethical individuality. Such a policy, whose consequences will probably one day be fatal for the Western world, is creating profound disarray in all the countries of Asia and Africa. It has been incapable of producing any ethical or religious substitute that would be valid for the entire Indian population. There are consequently no grounds for considering this state of transitory disorder, of which Gandhism is one of the characteristic forms, as being either the outcome of the cosmological, religious, social, or ethical concepts of Hinduism, nor the result of their application to the problems of the modern world.

The Hindu Caste System

Il n'y a rien de barbare et de sauvage en cette nation,
sinon que chacun appelle barbarie
ce qui n'est pas de son usage.
[I do not find that there is anything barbaric or savage about this nation,
unless we are to call barbarism whatever differs from our own customs.]
MONTAIGNE, *ESSAIS*, 1580

The Indian caste system was created with the aim of allowing widely different races, civilizations, and cultural and religious entities to survive and coexist. It has been working for close to 4000 years, with remarkable results. Whatever its faults, this essential goal should not be forgotten.

The fundamental principle of the caste institution is recognition of the right of any group to survive, to maintain its institutions, its beliefs, religion, language, and culture, and the right of each race to establish itself, meaning the right of the child to continue its line of descent, to benefit from its genetic heritage, refined through a long series of ancestors. This implies a prohibition of mixing, or procreation between different races and cultural entities.

"The principle of all life, of all progress, of all energy, lies in differences, in contrasts," teaches Hindu cosmology. "Leveling is death,"

16

whether it concerns matter, life, society, or any form of energy. The whole natural world turns on the coexistence and interdependence of species and their varieties. Even today, one of the characteristics of the Indian world is the variety of human types—their beauty, pride, style, "race"—at all levels of society.

Left alone, any human group will organize itself according to its tastes, aptitudes, and needs. Since these vary, liberty and equality essentially mean respecting such differences. Any social justice worthy of the name has to uphold not only the right of each individual, but also the right of each human group, to live according to its nature, whether innate or acquired, within the framework of its linguistic, cultural, ethical, and religious heritage, forming the protective matrix needed for the harmonious development of its personality. All attempts at leveling are based on the concepts of a dominant group and lead inevitably to the destruction of other groups' values, to their enslavement, and to the physical, spiritual, or mental crushing of the weak. In return, the latter—if they are assimilated in sufficient numbers—take their revenge by gradually sapping the virtues and institutions of those who have accepted or enslaved them. This is how empires come to an end.

In a society that is not racially and culturally homogeneous, political power can only survive by respecting the autonomy, character, and beliefs of the various ethnic groups. Ancient Indian texts—such as *The Laws of Manu (Manu Smriti)*, Shukra's *Politics (Shukraniti)*, and, somewhat later, the *Artha Shastra* by Kautilya—have established rules defining the duties and privileges of the various ethnic and professional groups in a multiracial society. This system is known as Varnashram, "The Caste Institution."

CASTE, PROFESSION, BEHAVIOR CODES, AND CULTURE

The development of complex civilization made it essential to attribute to each caste and ethnic group a basic profession that would ensure the survival of its members, which was forbidden to the other castes. At a professional level, the castes are divided into four main groups, corresponding to the four essential functions, which are:

> Brahmans, scholar-priests
> Kshatriyas, warriors and kings
> Vaishyas, tradesmen and farmers
> Shudras, artisans and laborers

Europe experienced a similar division with Church, Nobility, and Third-Estate. Vestiges of this remain in the Army, the *Nomenclature*, and workers' unions.

Castes and Corporations

The right to work, essential in every ordered society, implies corporative privilege. We have an example of this in modern Sweden, where you haven't even the right to repair your lock or electric oven by yourself, thus depriving the locksmith and electrician of their job.

The organization of a multiracial society implies the formation of corporations—basic trades set aside for different groups and suited to their aptitudes—which guarantee them their livelihood. Thus, in the Christian and Muslim world, Jews have long assumed the professions of bankers and musicians. The notion of any hierarchy of professions is a modern idea. One trade is like another. Social balance means that all functions must be respected and the stability of the family trade guaranteed by the corporation. In France, we know to what extent miners are attached to their trade and way of life, extending to their resistance to being requalified for jobs that are considered much less arduous.

Organizing social groups as corporations gives them importance, pride, and a power that is much greater than that of the composite and anonymous trade unions, easily manipulated by political forces in ways that are often contrary to their true interests.

With its traditions of technology, ethics, and solidarity, the corporation is a factor that is at least as important as nationality, which is a matter of territory, language, and—eventually—of religion. A musician or skilled artisan can easily change nationality, because he remains a member of his corporation. An unskilled person will find no niche for himself and will automatically become an outcaste. This problem involves all non-selective emigration.

In any profession organized as a corporation, social mobility is possible. According to Indian theory, the manager of a shoe factory must belong, on principle, to the shoemaker's caste. Caste has nothing to do with wealth.

Duties and Privileges

Each caste, each coherent human group, has a code of behavior, customs, and virtues that are peculiar to it. To prevent any one caste from taking all the privileges, it is essential that each group, beside its cultural, religious, and linguistic originality, should be given certain advantages as well as certain restrictions. This leads to a theory of equivalences that opposes the notion of equality. Interestingly, the higher the rank in society, the more severe the moral obligations and restrictions. *Noblesse oblige.*

A Brahman may own few material goods, may practice no manual profession, nor engage in trade. He cannot divorce and cannot, without losing prestige, drink alcohol or smoke, and must observe very strict dietary rules. He cannot travel abroad, has to practice constant ablutions, may touch no one outside his family members. He is the only real untouchable. He can neither sell knowledge, nor teach for money, so that he cannot teach at modern universities. He may, however, receive gifts.

A member of the Kshatriya caste has the knightly duty of courage, justice, endurance, and honor. Warriors are not vegetarians. A warrior may have a harem, but may not engage in trade, nor practice any manual labor. A prince-musician may play for his friends, but he may not give a public concert, nor may he play for a fee on the radio. A member of the princely caste of knights who lacks courage, who is feeble and cowardly, who does not defend the weak against extortion, is a dishonor to his caste. Parallels of knightly chivalry can also be found in the West.

Vaishyas, tradesmen and landowners, are responsible for food production and trade. It is they who ensure the state's finances. It is their duty to subsidize the temples, religious orders, and charitable institutions. An echo of this can be seen in those American foundations set up by the very rich. As a rule, Vaishyas are devout, puritanical people.

The Shudras—artisans and laborers—form the majority of the population. They are shoemakers, weavers, boatmen, raisers of cattle. They also include what we term artists, musicians, painters, and sculptors, as well as the ancient tribes surviving from the Stone Age, who are hunter-gatherers, practicing rudimentary farming and occasionally hiring out their services. The Shudras are divided into numerous professional groups, which are highly independent and often of different ethnic origins.

A member of the artisan castes enjoys advantages of which he is very conscious. He can have several wives, divorce, smoke, take drugs. The Shudra never envies the poor Brahman, respected but crippled by restrictions. When they quarrel, the Ganges boatmen threaten each other with the words, "By my curse you will be reborn as a Brahman and will no longer be able to drink or fornicate." As a rule, a Shudra is not a vegetarian unless he wishes to study and follow the teaching of scholars. In such a case, he must, for a time, observe the same rules as a Brahman student. Except for this eventuality, he has no dietary restrictions other than that of not eating the meat of bovines, which are sacred animals and cannot be killed. (The few wretched groups who do eat beef are consequently outcastes, and are rejected by society.)

Pariahs or Untouchables

Persons whose profession is deemed to be unclean—in a society that attaches great importance to contamination and purifications—are subject to sometimes severe restrictions. Such persons include refuse collectors, tanners (who handle animal corpses), and gravediggers.

The word *pariah*, which means "drum-player," is of Portuguese origin, taken from the Tamil *parai*, the large drum played during festivals. This is an unclean profession because the drum head is of leather, coming from an animal corpse. In actual fact, there are not many Pariahs, and they should not be confused with the other artisan castes. In town planning, one district is set aside for artisans, but street sweepers, tanners, and gravediggers must live outside the walls, as was once the case for the hangman in Europe.

The squalid districts created in large cities by an industrial civilization pose similar problems that appear difficult to solve, whether in India or the West. This question is separate from caste groupings.

The Council of Five: The Panchayat

Since each group has its own laws, customs, ethical concepts, and various taboos, breaches cannot be judged by persons from other groups. Each caste elects its own local panchayat, or "Council of Five," which judges all the group's internal affairs: theft, breach of confidence, gaming debts, brawls, inheritance, conjugal infidelity, divorce, rape, and so on. The state courts only take cognizance of murder cases or disputes between castes that the local panchayats cannot settle.

This kind of organization makes it possible to create within each group, however humble, high judicial functions and officials who confirm their autonomy and the solidity of their ethical values and institutions. In the West, freemasonry is a survival of the ethical and spiritual ideal of a corporation of temple builders. We tend to hark back to a similar principle with our arbitrators and mediators. The problems experienced by jury members having to judge persons from other castes was pointed out by Kinsey in his famous report.

Profession and Culture

The caste theory lays great emphasis on the difference between profession and culture. The corporation's executives try to assure that everyone has a trade, a livelihood, the right to work. Culture itself—the search for learning, knowledge, the individual's intellectual development—is a personal question that implies no change in social status. What is important is to raise the cultural level of the population as a whole, even when certain branches of teaching are tied to particular corporations. The teaching of the thirty-two sciences and sixty-four arts—as mentioned in sociological and political texts—is divided among the castes.

Thus, the teaching of philosophy, astronomy-astrology, and mythology is reserved to the Brahmans, medicine being practiced by a lower Brahman caste. The raising of horses and elephants, the technology of weapons and war machines, and the driving of chariots (nowadays automobiles) are warrior crafts. This is why poor Sikhs, belonging to the warrior caste, are taxi-drivers, just like the Russian princes in exile.

As stated above, arts and crafts—such as music, sculpture, painting, poetry, weaving, pottery, and so on—belong to the artisans or Shudras, and persons from other castes may not practice these arts professionally. The same goes for dancing and the theatre, trades set aside as professions for courtesans (*devadasi*) and homosexual prostitutes (*shanda*). People from top society cannot practice these trades. It was the same in Europe only a short while ago.

Anyone can study philosophy, metaphysics, music, painting, or dancing as an art for pleasure, but cannot practice it as a trade without losing prestige. A great part of the literary and poetic tradition is transmitted by bards who chant the legends of the *Ramayana*, the *Mahabharata*, and the *Bhagavata*, as well as mystic poems, such as *Bhajana*, *Kirtana*, and so on. They belong to the artisan castes, like musicians. Some of them have become famous and their names have gone down in history, like Jayadeva and Kabir.

Special Aptitudes

For persons with a special aptitude for study, literature, or for the arts, caste is not an obstacle. An artist, poet, or writer is honored by the whole of society, whatever his origin, but his personal status does not change his caste and cannot be transmitted to his children, who will remain princes or shoemakers. Talent is not a value that can be inherited. Artists are received everywhere, among the middle classes or in aristocratic circles, which does not mean that they are assimilated. No form of learning is closed to anyone. Only its commercialization is limited. A blacksmith can study philosophic texts, but cannot practice the trade of the priest or teacher, unless he renounces marriage, the creation of a family, and his caste.

I was able to integrate myself into Hindu society because, being interested in music, I entered by the door of the humble. As a Shudra respecting the hierarchy, I could study musical art with artisan musicians. But I was also able to study mythology, cosmology, and metaphysics with the Brahmans, which is impossible for a proud European who rejects his status as a mleccha (untouchable barbarian) and claims to be a Roman Brahman, as did the Jesuits in the eighteenth century.

Racial Pride

A characteristic feature of any human group is being proud of belonging to a species. Survivals of this can be found in national and religious pride—pride at being French or Breton, Christian or Muslim—a pride that has nothing to do with the merits of the group in the eyes of outsiders.

As with all animal species, children are always proud of their group and accept the physical, cultural, and religious ideal of the society into which they are born. Even nowadays in India, it is rare to encounter a person who is not proud of his caste, or who would like to belong to another group, just as one rarely meets a Frenchman who wants to be a German, even if he is a violent critic of the French character and social system. The same goes for religious groups, which are also hereditary.

A young Brahman, a disciple of Gandhi, decided to demonstrate his rejection of caste by marrying a sweeper's very pretty daughter. Her mother arrived indignant and threatened Gandhi with her broom, saying, "My daughter will marry an honest boy from her own caste, never one of your corrupt Brahmans!"

CASTE AND SEXUALITY

The continuation of the species, of the race, is a profound instinct bound up with the reproductive functions. Normal reproductive instinct signifies indifference to any partner who does not belong to the same species. According to Darwin, the only objective of the genes is to produce copies of themselves. Organisms and individuals are only their agents. With the appearance of interracial unions, we enter the domain of perversions of this instinct.

It would clearly be ideal to consult the baby before its birth to know whether it prefers to be born white, black, Catholic, Jew, Protestant, or half-breed, artisan, or middleclass. Since this is not possible, he has to be satisfied with the heredity he receives at birth. Social responsibility consists in making this heredity the most harmonious possible, the most true to race, the best suited to the *raison d'être* of the individual and social person.

In traditional Hindu society, marriage is not merely a license to have sexual relations. It is a responsible act, sanctioned by society, whose aim is to transmit the genetic heritage, built up through the long line of ancestors, to new beings, who will thus be suitable to continue the particular human type, culture, civilization, way of life, and profession. Marriages are arranged during childhood, taking into account factors of caste, race, the degree of consanguinity, as well as physical characteristics and social environment, with the concordance of horoscopes, and so on. Financial matters and physical attraction are not taken into account. Only criteria deemed to favor the children to be born are considered. I attended the marriage of one of the most eligible women in India, the daughter of an immensely rich and powerful maharajah, whose dynasty goes back to the pre-Aryan period. The only husband who could be found for her was the son of an aged dethroned kinglet, living wretchedly in the Himalayas, but belonging to the same racial group.

Child marriages, so often decried, do not as a rule pose any problems. A boy of ten knows that there is a little girl who is his wife, just as he has a mother, whom he has not chosen either. The marriage is often consummated at around fifteen, when sexual curiosity is not very selective. At the same time, husband and wife do not live as a couple, but within the wider family group. Men and women form separate entities. Infidelities within the group may create personal problems, but do not affect the genetic heritage, or concern society.

Infertility

If his wife is barren, it is a man's duty to take a second wife. In the case of the man's infertility, the couple may engage a sturdy and well-made young Brahman (Brahmans are considered to be the purest race). "After the end of the woman's period and the customary purifications, the Brahman practices ritual copulation with her" (a kind of *hierogamy*). If a child is born, it is deemed legitimate.

Suttee (Sati)

Consecrated marriage is an indissoluble union. A woman who has had sexual relations with a man is transformed by that union. This is why the remarriage of widows is forbidden among the higher castes. The widow continues to live with the other women within the family group, but must not have other children. Some widows leave their family and retire to monastic life.

The Scythes and Mongols, warrior peoples who migrated from Asia at a fairly late period, sacrificed the wives, servants, and horses of a dead warrior, so that they could accompany him in his afterlife. Assimilated Scythes introduced among the warrior caste the rite whereby a widow without children let herself be burned on her husband's funeral pyre. This deed is known as *sati* (act of faith), and is deemed highly meritorious, belonging to the heroic virtues of the princely caste. It is not practiced by other castes. Similarly, the wives of the Rajput princes vanquished by the Muslims, at various times, committed collective suicide in a room that was set on fire, so as to avoid falling into the invaders' hands. The practice of sati is unknown in the ancient texts on caste duties.

The Gods' Handmaidens

Erotic play is an important element in human equilibrium. Women seeking sexual freedom instead of maternity join a group known as "the

Gods' Handmaidens" (devadasi), for whom dancing and music are set aside as professions. They form a highly honored corporation. The bond between theater callings and courtesans is not peculiar to India. Homosexuals and transvestites, whether prostitutes or not, form a separate group and enjoy certain privileges, especially in religious plays. In both cases, they are specialized corporations, their members coming from different castes.

They are considered as outcastes with recognized rights, but do not take part in the continuation of the different races, corporations, and castes. It is considered essential that an adventure that only concerns affective and erotic relations and has no reproductive goal should remain sterile. Giving birth to a child that has no place in society is seen as an extremely serious moral fault. Plant extracts causing abortion or used as anticonception prophylaxis are widely used and very efficacious in Indian medicine.

The freedom of pleasure, in any form, is essential to the development of the individual. Reproduction is something else and the two must not be confused. Out of the several million spermatozoids that a man produces during the course of his life, only a few serve for reproduction. The only valid ethic concerns these few, which are to continue the species and contribute to its progress. All the rest are dispersed as pleasure demands. In our increasingly hybrid societies, it is sometimes difficult to find partners whose genetic characteristics are sufficiently close to assure a homogeneous, balanced, and harmonious progeny.

From a Hindu point of view, the Christian concept of the love marriage that sanctifies a sexual union arising from erotic or sentimental attraction, without taking into account the quality of its product—the child and its genetic heritage—or its insertion into society, is a moral and social aberration. Love and sexual pleasure in all their forms are a matter of the individual's personal satisfaction and as such are perfectly recommendable. Producing bastards is an antisocial and inhuman act that must be avoided, even in animals. Hybrids, the result of a mixture of races, are, according to Hindu theory, a step backward to a stage that is the more primitive the further apart the groups that mix are from each other. Individuals of mixed race possess neither the aptitudes, moral virtues, nor intellectual qualities of the groups from which they have come. They form unstable entities, difficult to control and to utilize.

Children who possess none of their parents' characteristics contest the latters' customs and are hostile to their virtues. It is impossible for them to take over their parents' functions and thus their livelihood is at risk. The family tends to dissolve. Mixed societies are ungovernable, since the family problem equally affects the group—which loses its solidarity—and finally, the nation, which becomes an incongruous assembly of ill-assorted individuals, without cohesion, without any logical groupings, struggling perpetually to survive. According to the *Puranas*, the mixture of races and castes is one of the warning signs of the destruction of humanity.

Monks

Exceptional individuals may become attached to the monastic tradition of the renouncer, the Sannyasi, which is open to all. Hindu monks do not live in monasteries. They lead an independent life and form a parallel occult society. It is through them that the highest forms of knowledge are transmitted.

When certain aspects of doctrine appear to be in danger in the Brahman family tradition—since intelligence and character are not necessarily hereditary—they are taken from them. They are then transmitted by the Sannyasis, the wandering monks, no longer from father to son, but from master to disciple, and only after the disciple has managed to pass the tests that allow him to be considered qualified. Thus, in certain regions of India, the Brahmans currently transmit the memory of the texts and the Sannyasis their meaning.

A Sannyasi receives a new name. His caste of origin is abolished. Eroticism and sensuality are not necessarily forbidden him, but he may not found a family. Sometimes a Sannyasi has a female companion, a *Shakti*, or a young male companion. According to the *Puranas*, taking in wandering monks for no reward is one of the moral duties of prostitutes.

ASSIMILATED GROUPS

Some homogenous groups of half-breeds form separate categories, sorts of new castes for which a place must be found. Such groups include the *Nayyar*s of Kerala, the outcome of the mixture of Aryan Brahmans and Dravidian women during the Aryan colonization of southern India. The same thing occurred with invaders and refugees: the Scythes, Parthians, Greeks, Parsis, Christians, Buddhists. Nowadays the Tibetans have found in India a land of refuge where they can survive while maintaining their autonomy, beliefs, culture, and race.

Human groups that have been persecuted or eliminated everywhere else live and prosper in India and even, when they have the ability, manage to play a leading role in the nation's affairs, as do the Parsis. The Jewish and Christian communities, which have been settled for nearly two thousand years, have never encountered the slightest problem, or experienced the least persecution or xenophobia. The primitive tribes, still living in the Stone Age, have never—until our own times—been disturbed.

The incorporation of immigrants or new communities implies looking for and guaranteeing them some employment or job, while respecting their autonomy, and avoiding those mixtures that give rise to the reactions of rejection. The Parsi refugees from Iran have been associated with the merchant caste; the Scythes and Parthians have formed warrior castes: the Jats. Anglo-Indian half-breeds, usually the result of British soldiers and low caste Indian women (at the time when, before the opening of the Suez Canal, English women did not accompany their men to the "colonies"), have been allotted employment on the railways, which were created at the same period.

Modern society in official Delhi circles appears very open and very liberal. This does not mean that, in their private lives, families do not observe caste rules, especially as far as marriage, diet, and employment are concerned. Westernized Indians, even when they observe caste traditions, always fail to explain to foreigners what it is really about, for fear of being insulted. They have learned to say, as Indian domestic servants used to say, "It is an Indian product, Sahib; it's not worth anything."

The recent Sikh revolt, which led to the assassination of Indira Gandhi, arose from the refusal of the socialist government of India to respect the principle of their autonomy and from the decision to settle in their provinces hundred of thousands of Hindu refugees from Pakistan, in a rather similar manner to the French government's facilitating the settlement of the *pieds noirs* in Corsica. The respective merits of the two communities have nothing to do with the problem.

The development of each species is tied to its territory. According to Jacques Ruffié, "an animal does not reproduce until it has marked out its domain, delimited its territory."[1] The problem of racial coexistence is the creation, in one form or another, of an inviolable space assured to each community.

Anti-Caste Revolts

Revolts against caste groupings and hierarchy have taken place at various times. As in the case of the French Revolution, they arise in middleclass circles rather than among the masses. Such was the case of the revolt of the middleclass and princely castes against the power of the priests, which gave rise to the Buddhist heresy in the sixth century B.C.E.

In our own time, anti-caste movements have been organized by Indians raised in England, people of the merchant caste, like Gandhi, or outcaste Brahmans, like Nehru, whereas the artisans have joined the Brahmans to defend the established order and maintain their identity, their way of life, and their caste pride.

Clearly, abuses are found in Indian society, as in all societies. Such abuses have, in the past, been exaggeratedly stigmatized and have increased considerably since successive governments, Muslim and Christian, have sought to ignore the castes and have not respected their related privileges and restrictions. Since the caste system was not recognized by the central government, it was clearly in no position to adapt to modern conditions, which it would have done had it been left alone. At the same time, there have never been any problems in the princely states.

The effect of the abolition of the castes, theoretically imposed by the Congress Government since Independence, has largely been that of allowing persons belonging to the privileged castes to seize the professions and lands of the humbler classes.

Thus, the tribes have been dispossessed of their territories and reduced to famine, and the international stage is filled with Brahman musicians and dancers who are the daughters of rich merchants, while their masters remain in the shade. One exception has been the players of oboes and drums, who, since their instruments are unclean, still belong to the artisan castes, to the greater benefit of musical art.

THE PERMANENCE OF THE CASTES

Human beings need to group themselves on the basis of their race, tribe, function, language, territory, nation, and religion. This usually leads to conflicts, unless some form of coexistence is found. Whatever its faults, the Hindu caste system has over the ages prevented genocides, and found a place for all minorities, all ways of living, and all religions. The attempt to suppress the privileges of the various ethnic groups, in the name of an egalitarianism imported from the West, has led to the recent wars of religion, social conflicts, and tribal genocide in India.

According to the *Manu Smriti*, when caste divisions are threatened as a result of invasions, acculturation, and the mixing of races, they tend gradually to reappear on an aptitudinal basis, since they correspond to the nature of every ordered and effective society. Such new castes tend to become hereditary, a doctor's son becomes a doctor, a farmer's son a farmer. Five generations are needed to reconstitute a caste of Brahmans or intellectuals, but only two for an artisan caste.

Except in the case of highly homogenous human groups—human herds—no developed society can exist without a hierarchical division of functions, requiring different virtues, distinct professional ethics, and different living standards, all of which tend to become hereditary. This phenomenon is inherent in humankind, a universal aspect of social biology. Each animal species has its own particular social behavior.

Wherever the caste order has been destroyed by natural catastrophe, invasion, or revolution, it has always reappeared in one form or another.

Corporations have played a major role in the development of Western civilization. Freemasonry retains a shadowy reflection of this. Even today, trade guilds preserve the traditions, virtues, ethics, and nobility of the ancient corporations of artisans that built our cathedrals. Similar traditions lie at the root of Japan's strength.

Royal families still observe caste rules. Unsuitable alliances cause them to lose their rights, as in the case of Edward VIII of England.

Among the masses, inter-class marriages are frowned upon and are one of the main causes of xenophobia.

THE END OF THE WORLD?

When, at the end of the Kali Yuga, the last age of the life cycle of this present human species, an irremediable mixture of races and castes takes place and the highest forms of knowledge fall into the hands of people who do not possess the corresponding moral virtues, humanity will cease to play its role and will be destroyed. The only way to avoid the great slaughter and destruction that looms is a return to the caste system, a respect for difference and race, which is the work of the Creator.

In the modern world, this need for a return to the natural order is felt, and the right to be different is appearing in marginal areas, as well as among some ethnic groups that are asserting themselves—such as Israelis, Palestinians, Kurds, Armenians, and Blacks—and refusing to be assimilated. "Black is beautiful" is an expression coined by Black Americans to confirm this instinct.

Indeed, at every period of history, we see the reappearance of castes, corporations, and hierarchies, and restrictions on inter-group marriage.

According to the Hindus, the world does not develop by chance. It develops according to a plan, like the individual, from the ovum to the adult. The social characteristics of cultured humans are part of the plan for the species. Human types inevitably develop to suit the various essential functions, in order to accomplish humanity's role in the world. Society forms a protective shell, within which the highest forms of understanding and knowledge can blossom, making the human being a privileged witness of the divine work. A world that is not perceived does not exist. Knowledgeable man is a mirror in which the Creator can contemplate his work and realize himself. Human society must succeed in forming the framework within which certain people can develop increasingly refined forms of knowledge and perception of the nature of the universe.

Racism and Castes

WHAT IS RACISM?

Race relations can be established in four different ways: by domination, elimination, assimilation, or coexistence.

Starting probably from the Biblical concept of a human species originating from a single couple, some Western geneticists—in order to gratify fashionable ideologies—claim to demonstrate that the aptitudes of the various human races are identical and equal, leading to the imposition of the values of a particular civilization that is deemed superior.

Democratic ideology finds it difficult to let different ethnic groups coexist without being destroyed or assimilated. Egalitarian principles lead either to the elimination of the recalcitrant or to their theoretical assimilation, transforming them, in actual fact, into second-class citizens, which is a subtle, or more pernicious, form of genocide.

The fact of being different does not mean being inferior, except in the order of values of the dominant group. The right to be different is a fundamental right of both species and individuals. All tyrannical regimes seek to level human beings, the better to exploit them. Ecological dramas find their origin in the human race's claimed superiority over other animal and vegetable species.

Viable results cannot be reached starting from false assumptions. First we must clearly define on what level human beings can be considered equal, since they are evidently not alike. To define absurd generalizations belonging to what the Hindus call "the metaphysics of imbeciles" (*anadhikari vedanta*), the following classical example is used: "Before God, all beings are equal. Therefore my mother, my wife, and my daughter are equal, and I can consequently sleep with all three."

Egalitarianism is used as an excuse for destroying cultural values, the knowledge, social virtues, and metaphysical conceptions belonging to the heritage of the various human groups. They are gradually eliminated, just as we stupidly eliminate innumerable varieties of plants and animals that we are unable to domesticate for our own use, whose disappearance we deplore too late.

The history of the West is merely a long succession of invaders eliminating the autochthonous peoples and minorities, and destroying the temples of the vanquished.

True antiracism can only be founded on respect for differences in both the individual and the collectivity, whether it is a question of racial, cultural, linguistic, ethnic, social, moral, or religious values, or aptitudes for technology, philosophy, dancing, or mathematics. What is essential is the right of each to be black, yellow, or white; Muslim, animist, Christian, Jewish, or atheist; polygamist, monogamist, matriarchal, patriarchal, or homosexual; vegetarian or carnivore; artisan or intellectual; without being ceaselessly confronted with a standardized model, which can only be that of a given period in a given civilization. The solution put forward today in the name of antiracism implies a suppression of the problem, feigning to ignore aptitudinal differences between races, and seeking to create a uniform humanity of half-castes, which, in the name of egalitarian principles, leads to the discreet destruction of races, individuals, and communities that cannot or do not wish to adapt themselves to this hybrid model.

Equality can only be promoted by suppressing those who are less equal than others in the framework of a particular civilization which is proclaimed to be the best and which must be imposed on all "for their own good." The example of the Hutu tribes in Rwanda—who cut off the legs of the tallest Tutsis to reduce them to the height of the majority—is an extreme and absurd expression of the notion of equality.

The modern world practices wide-scale elimination of peoples surviving from prehistoric times, who cannot adapt to the conditions of our civilizations. We witness the rapid destruction of non-assimilable peoples, such as the Gonds and the Santals in India, the Aborigines in Australia, the Pygmies, the Polynesians, the ancient peoples of America. In the name of an egalitarianism imported from the West, they are dispossessed, exploited, and then assassinated, since—whatever is asserted about the equality of humankind—it is not possible to make an atomic scientist or a factory worker out of a Gond or Pygmy, nor a one-hundred-meters Olympic champion out of a Japanese. A community of Sioux, Bushmen, or Eskimos dies wretchedly when a way of life to which its members are not suited is imposed upon them, together with unequal competition in a society that is not their own. At the most, for a certain time, zoological gardens of "scientific" interest, known as "reserves" are set up for rare specimens of Iroquois or Australian Aborigines, while no effort is spared to Christianize them to ensure their dependence. An analysis of the reasoning and statements of the antiracists highlights their incoherence: they are often the most perfidious enemies of the threatened groups, races, and civilizations. They are also often manipulated by economic interests that utilize antiracism as a means for subjecting the threatened peoples and confiscating their territories.

What is termed antiracism today as a rule implies reducing the human species to the Western way of life, which Westerners deem to be the best and most developed. The antiracist ideal is to clothe the Congolese, Chinese, or Indians in a suit, as can be seen at international meetings. Otherwise, they find no audience, have no right to respect, are considered to be primitive, the subject of amused interest. An African is "civilized" if he wears a Cardin suit and speaks "excellent French or English." You never encounter antiracists who speak excellent Swahili or Bengali and wear a *boubou* or a *dhoti*, except as a carnival disguise. A female Breton member of parliament who wears her headdress in the Chamber will be treated as a naïve country girl. Soviet egalitarianism speaks Russian.

SEX AND RACISM

Sexuality appears to play a fundamental role in racist or antiracist attitudes.

The violence of white Americans toward the Blacks, who are sexually better endowed, betrays an inferiority complex. Such a feeling may even take the opposite tack of a taste for masochistic submission. The difference in American attitudes toward the Indians and the Blacks is characteristic. The Indians inspire no sexual jealousy. Their extermination is merely a matter of banditry—of eliminating them in order to appropriate their lands—a process that continues today. White American attitudes toward Blacks smack much more of sadism: beatings, torture, burning alive, the death penalty for any Black who seduces a white woman, whereas Whites could freely sleep with their slaves, producing a considerable number of Black-Scots, Black-Dutch, and Black-Frenchmen. The most fanatical and arrogant racists, like the American pioneers, never worry about procreating with their slaves, or even abandoning their progeny. This puritanical antifeminine racism also raises its head in the persecution of homosexuals by the "superior" variety of male, who is probably not so sure of his masculinity. Such an attitude is never encountered in a Don Juan.

Whether it is a question of Whites wanting to marry Blacks, or Blacks with a taste for White women, no one worries about the result, the generalization of hybrids, which is even presented as genetic progress.

MIXING RACES

With the spread of crossbreeding, we are seeing a great part of the human race's genetic heritage gradually disappear. The case is similar for domesticated animal species and plants, where stocks tend to disappear in favor of hybrids, as geneticists are noticing with some anxiety. The decreased number of distinct stocks deprives the hybrids of the possibility of renewal in the event of attack. The European vine-stock, destroyed by phylloxera, could only be reconstituted thanks to American plants.

What is an established fact for all living species has no reason to be denied in the case of humankind. As Professor Albert Jacquard recently remarked, it is essential "to recover the diversity of species that our 'improvements' have made homogeneous, i.e. impoverished."

The instinct to reject and eliminate hybrids, which is called racism, is thus a normal defense mechanism of the social body, similar to the rejection of grafted organs by any living organism. By means of an aberration typical of the modern world, we may observe that a society that stigmatizes a worker who betrays his union, and shoots "collaborators" who fraternize with the invader, tends to encourage those who betray their species by giving birth to half-breeds.

Like apartheid, the ghetto is a bad solution for avoiding racial crossbreeding, because it prevents the fruitful, free cooperation of the different communities in a given territory.

RACE AND CULTURE

Racial characteristics relate to certain forms of culture.

Modern hematologists confirm the singularity of the Cambodian people, many of whom have a special hemoglobin—hemoglobin E—in their blood. The area covered by hemoglobin E can be superimposed on the area covered by the monuments of the Khmer culture.[1]

CULTURAL HYBRIDIZATION

Study of the cultural heritage established over the centuries by each ethnic group, tied as a rule to a particular language, represents a considerable enrichment for culture as a whole. All true culture is polyglot, while, on the other hand, linguistic and cultural hybridization is destructive.

Having lived as long in the traditional Hindu civilization as I have in Western Judeo-Christian society, I am aware to what extent the cultural values of either society can be contradictory and cancel each other.

In seeking to discover more about the metaphysical, cosmological, and semantic concepts of the ancient culture of India, I sometimes have the impression of reaching the limits of my own intelligence, of my faculty of understanding, whereas I have learned nothing from Hindus with modern training. Westernized Hindus are mediocre and superficial on the level of both cultures, as are also those Westerners who frequent ashrams. There are, of course, exceptions. Some people can transfer from one culture to another, just as there are people who change sex, but they are rare cases and cannot be used as a basis for generalization.

THE COLONIZING MISSION

Thanks to the egalitarianism sanctioned by Buddhism and adopted by the princely class, India saw a considerable colonial expansion starting from the third century B.C.E. Buddhist monks, together with families of Brahmans, princes, merchants, and artisans, were exported to the peripheral areas—Bengal and southern India, and even as far as Indochina and Indonesia—their religious mission serving as a pretext for colonial exploitation. Everywhere, the occupiers assumed prerogatives, taking over the professions reserved for the different castes, a practice that was to develop much later, at the time of Muslim and European domination, giving rise to rapid decadence and mass revolts.

We have recently witnessed in Cambodia a double form of racism: on the one hand, the extermination, by means of internal "purges," of social groups deemed not assimilable by an imported ideology, and on the other, domination by a foreign people aiming at the gradual elimination of the language, culture, and identity of the survivors in the name of the same ideology. The Soviets were ready to annihilate three-quarters of the population of Afghanistan, considered not assimilable by Marxism, just as they had already done to other populations in the U.S.S.R.

The problem of the underdevelopment of certain peoples—to whom the West wishes to appear as a potential benefactor—is usually wrongly stated, being merely a commercial pretext for imposing an often harmful industrial surplus on regions and peoples that have no real need of it. This is part of a program to depersonalize traditional societies to the greater advantage of trade. A country is underdeveloped by comparison with whom and with what? Mrs. Montessori, the famous Italian child educationalist, during a trip to India at the beginning of the century, exclaimed with horror, "Che povertà! Non hanno neanche le scarpe!" (What poverty! They haven't even got shoes!) in a climate where wearing shoes is real torture.

All conquests and colonialism, all religious, ideological, linguistic, and cultural (i.e. ethical) propaganda are fundamentally destructive, as is the unilateral notion of progress. The missionary fanaticism of Christians, Muslims, and Marxists has always been and still is a tool of the over-powerful to depersonalize and subject both peoples and individuals. With rare exceptions, we are witnessing the gradual disappearance, beneath the steamroller of so-called Western egalitarianism, of the plastic arts, dance, music, traditional sciences, and even the languages of Africa and other continents.

Up to the middle of the twentieth century, the superiority of the white race, its civilization and religion, was considered as an indisputable fact in Europe. It needed the excesses of Nazism to challenge this assumption.

The conviction of the superiority of Europeans and of Christianity served as an excuse for colonial expansion. We feel a shiver of horror when, in 1984, we see the highest prelate of the Catholic Church celebrate the anniversary of the arrival of the Spanish in America, bearing the "Christian message," when we think of the genocide it served to cover and the current status of Indians in so-called "Latin" America.

Christianity is theoretically antiracist, so long as everyone becomes a Christian and obeys the church's arbitrary dogmas. Islam is also antiracist, if you become a Muslim. Marxism is antiracist, so long as you accept its principles, ethics, and class-racism. These three ideologies have sought to create religious and social conflict in India. Antiracists use against their own race a racism that others practice on their neighbors. Both attitudes are equally arbitrary and suicidal. The fanaticism that characterizes these ideologies has often led to catastrophe. The sack of Rome by Christianized barbarians occurred because a young Christian girl opened the gate of the city to them. In the name of blind idealism, local Communists have often delivered their country up to the Soviet invader.

The irrational nature of the notion of racism is clear, as shown by the fact that it is often associated with anti-Semitism, which is its opposite. One of the main virtues of the Jews (who are not the only Semites) is precisely their sense of belonging to a race, a peculiar people, and of keeping its unity, integrity, and beliefs. Respect for the racial and cultural autonomy of the Jews has nothing to do with the will to assimilate, and to negate differences, which antiracists promote in relation to other communities. What the Jews are reproached for is their refusal to be assimilated, their will to maintain their identity, just as, to a lesser extent, the Basques, Corsicans, or Bretons are reproached for the same thing.

Any so-called antiracism that makes no provision for a society where racial, linguistic, and religious groupings can cooperate within the framework of the nation, without losing their identity or being assimilated, is merely a form of colonialism. There would be no Jewish problem if, within each country, there existed a respected and recognized autonomous Jewish community. The same is valid for all minorities. It is quite possible to delegate responsibility to a centralized state authority for certain common interests, without abandoning the beliefs, way of life, and social system of each group.

THE ANTIRACIST TERROR

Among the incantations that play a hypnotic role in the verbal magic of our times and are used to manipulate public opinion to such an extent that their ambiguity lends them a sacred tone, the word "racism" ranks in the front line. This term also often confuses the recognition of different human families that have distinctive physical characteristics and aptitudes with the realities of civilization, religion, ethics, and customs, which may merely represent ways of life, or a precious cultural heritage.

The fear of infringing taboos concerning the blasphemous use of forbidden words means that the greatest thinkers, sociologists, biologists, psychologists, and historians employ astonishing circumlocutions to avoid being accused of racist heresy, which would immediately condemn their work. This is very apparent in works such as *Le Sang et l'Histoire* by Jean Bernard. The American publisher of one of my works asked me to suppress an important quotation from the *Vishnu Purana*, which would have tarred me with the suspicion of racism, whereas I am clearly not responsible for a text that is more than two thousand years old.

Any system that strives to recognize and respect the proper qualities, virtues, traditions, and autonomy of the various human groups, races, religions, and cultures and to grant to the various human societies the right to be different, to prevent minorities from being persecuted, flattened, or converted by the majority, sees the three imperialisms—Christian, Islamic, and Marxist—rise against it in the name of an egalitarianism that is simply a tool for domination, genocide, and generalized mediocrity. The racism that justifies conquest, slavery, and the elimination of peoples and cultures, and the sort of antiracism that promotes assimilation and the negation of differences are, in fact, two faces of the same imperialism.

The stereotyped descriptions of Indian society that we have inherited were invented in the nineteenth century to justify colonialism and its benefits. They must be considered cautiously. Many of the problems of modern India are the result of Islamic and Christian proselytism, employed to destroy the traditional concepts of social justice. In India, as in Europe, certain more or less Marxist individuals currently use the pretext of the wretchedness of the less-favored classes—largely created by an industrial civilization—in order to destroy society instead of seeking to improve the conditions of its disinherited sections. Social injustice exists everywhere, together with people that are despised or wretched, ineffective or good-for-nothing. There is no evidence that its proportion in India is greater than elsewhere. Hindu society cannot be judged by the industrial areas of Bombay or by the immense camp for refugees from Bangladesh that Calcutta has become after the partition of India.

Is India racist? Clearly it is so, from the point of view of Western permissiveness, because it is against racial mixtures, against marriage between different communities, and is only interested in the quality of the child's genetic heritage. At the same time, it is the only truly antiracist country, since it has allowed all races, all religions, and all communities to coexist harmoniously for thousands of years, making place for, and ensuring the survival of, all the peoples and religions that are persecuted elsewhere.

The Hindu Woman and the Goddess

When the first creative tendency appears in the neutral, inert, unpolarized substrate, it is already in the form of a current, a tension between two opposing poles. This dualism—which is the essence of all mental or physical existence—can be represented as a male principle and a female principle, penetrating everything. It is the nature of all form, all thought, all life. There is no question of priority or anteriority between the two poles, whose opposition causes the birth of thought and matter. One cannot exist without the other. According to Shaivite texts, Shiva, the male principle, without its "i"—which is its *shakti*, its power, the female principle—is but a corpse, *shava*, that is, a return to the neutral state of the non-manifest substrate.

The opposition of the male and female principles appears in all degrees of manifestation. No atom, no element, no form, no substance, no being can exist except as its expression. These two principles, eternally united and inseparable, which exist only through each other, are at the same time totally opposed, totally contrary, and wholly irreconcilable. Total masculinity, like total femininity, is entirely absent from the manifest, from the existing world. Logically, therefore, both one and the other can be taken as symbols of transgression beyond the cycle of life, of the total liberation of the being, of a return to the unpolarized substrate. There are thus two opposite ways of liberation: the male way and the female way, Shiva and Shakti. We are led to these two ways by those aspects of the manifest in which their opposition is most marked, their form most fully apparent, like day and night, the sexual organs, sensual pleasure and abstinence, the light of knowledge and the darkness of non-thought.

Whatever is between the poles of absolute masculinity and femininity proceeds from one and from the other. Everything that exists possesses to a different degree this double nature, now male, now female. The hermaphrodite is consequently the image of the created, of divine manifestation. The differentiation of beings and things is due to the degree of masculinity and femininity in their components. As a result, in the complex relationships of the world of form, each aspect, each being, is male or female in relation to another aspect, another state of being.

Applied to human society, this principle means that each degree on the scale is feminine or masculine as compared to the next degree higher or lower. Thus, the king is feminine as compared to the priest and is consequently subject to the latter; the merchant is feminine as compared to the king and pays homage to him; the artisan is feminine as compared to the merchant and serves him like a slave. The army, *sena*, is the sole spouse of Skanda, the virgin adolescent, the god of beauty and commander of the gods' army. The ascetics and sages who saw the god Rama in the forest obtained from him, as the fruit of their sacrifices, the boon of being reborn as shepherdesses, so as to become his lovers when he returned to earth in the form of Krishna, the incarnation of love.

The degree of masculinity or femininity in each being determines its role, its function. In order to comply with his own nature and realize his potential, each has to determine his position with regard to those he meets, thus realizing his dharma, a word that simply means "conforming to what one is." A man who is anxious to free himself from the slavery of existence must first and foremost know himself, so that he can conform to his own nature and then free himself from it. At the level of human society, male and female duties are fundamentally, irremediably opposed, and it is only when they follow contrary and complementary laws that these two human halves can fully realize themselves and be equal.

From an exoteric point of view, the male principle appears to be superior. Light, strength, sensuality, knowledge, and man dominate the night, grace, asceticism, intuition, and woman. That is why in the social order, woman is subject to man. She is his spouse, his slave, his companion, his complement, his shadow. In this role, she realizes herself and perfects herself, attaining by her submission what man has to earn by his strength. For woman, man is even a personification of the divine. She needs no other image. Her ritual consists of honoring this god. By venerating and serving her husband, she accomplishes her whole function, the total realization of her physical condition.

From an esoteric point of view, the female principle is predominant. In secret and magic rites, woman plays an essential and dominant role. Even in the external world, she rules over the home, the hidden inner cell, the sanctuary of which she is the goddess. A father performs the rites of initiation and caste for his sons, but it is their mother's blessing that is needed to start off on the secret way of *sannyasa*, renunciation.

To understand women's place in Hindu society, it must be remembered that the notion of material equality exists nowhere and at no level. Each being is born different from any other. In the almost infinite number of combinations of the components of a living being, it is practically unthinkable that the same arrangement can be reproduced, that two beings can be absolutely identical, with the same nature, the same appearance, the same function, the same rank. According to their characteristics, however, human beings can be classified in categories, to be realized by each one so as to attain the perfection of what he or she is, the sole path of inner progress.

Each person thus has to achieve perfection in a social or external role, as well as in a personal or inner role. These two roles may be profoundly different and even contradictory, such as with low-caste men who have to earn their livelihood at humble professions, but are at the same time sages, philosophers, saints, or artists, before whom kings and

Brahmans bow respectfully. This contradiction is particularly apparent in woman: simultaneously humble and exalted, slave and goddess, submissive wife and all-powerful mother.

Birth is not at all a matter of chance for Hindus, but the outcome of the degree of maturity of the transmigrating being. The circumstances of our birth correspond to the degree of development of our being, to the very conditions in which we can make our best progress. There is consequently no advantage in wishing to change status, function, in wishing to carry out another's duties. This is why—except in very rare borderline cases—one does not change sex or species, race or caste during one's lifetime.

If, however, we wish to make exceptional progress, making every effort to free ourselves rapidly from the bonds of life, we may—whatever our degree of development, whatever our place in the human hierarchy that is the image of heavenly order—renounce our external activities and devote ourselves entirely to the identification of our transmigrating self with the cosmic self. This is the way of sannyasa, renunciation, which excludes almost every external activity, and any social role.

The external hierarchy of beings and things is, as a rule, the opposite of their inner order. Thus, in the Kali Yuga, the world age in which we are now living, the status of women and the status of the Shudras, or workers, are the most desirable since, through humility alone, mere devotion to a visible master, they can attain an outer perfection that facilitates inner development, freeing us from the heavy chains of life and leading us effortlessly toward the high spheres of felicity and knowledge. At the same time, the status of the Brahman, so noble and magnificent, is disastrous in this dark age, because it entails such severe disciplines, such difficult rituals, that failure is almost certain. The being who fails to accomplish his destiny falls back into the lower spheres, from which he can only emerge after interminable effort. It is therefore not at all a matter of chance if, over the past thousand years, all the major mystic poets, all the great saints of India, have been men of lowly birth, who could easily free themselves from their social and ritual responsibilities and devote themselves to their inner life.

So, now, toward the end of the cycle, we are approaching a reversal of values. *Shakta* rites, in which the female principle is predominant, are the only ones that are effective. Among the ruins of external hierarchies, we see the descent of the night of destruction and death, through which the female principle of transcendent knowledge appears triumphant in its darkness that is more splendid than a million suns.

In the exoteric society, meaning the social order that safeguards the transmission of the rites, the higher we get in the hierarchy, the more the male role is important and the role of women fades away. The male is the guardian of external order, the rites, the revealed texts, the knowledge handed down by our ancestors. The noblest of women, the priest's wife, is the most humble, the most modest, the most sacred, the most untouchable.

At the bottom of the hierarchy, on the other hand, woman predominates in the material order. She reigns, she owns. Man is merely an agent of fecundation, playing a secondary role. He devotes himself to the arts, to pleasures, devotions, to secret rites. This is why, while the family of the priest, or Brahman, is always patriarchal, the artisan's family is, to varying degrees, matriarchal. In some regions of India, the people and even the kings are subject to matriarchal law. Land, houses, and assets belong to women. The daughter inherits from her mother, while the men work, play, make war. Women, who issue from the earth and are close to it, are the guardians of the goods it grants.

In the esoteric order, the female role predominates. The priest worships the goddess and female symbols. The esoteric work of the greatest philosophers is devoted to the glorification of this principle. Initiations into the highest Sannyasi orders are shakta in form. At the same time, in the lower castes, where the female principle is externally dominant, esoterism is phallic. In the secret corporation rites, dances, ceremonies, symbols, and invocations emphasize the male aspect of the divine.

The androgynous man, who unites certain male and female aspects, has a particularly sacred character, because in some way he symbolizes the outcome of the union of the principles, the substance of wealth and life. He is consequently deemed to be of good omen, his presence is necessary in representing sacred mysteries and is deemed favorable during marriage ceremonies. There are, too, highly secret wholly homosexual rituals, connected with the rites of Ganapati and Skanda, Shiva's sons.

In all aspects of the manifest, pure form, the abstract concept of things, and the thought from which the cosmos and the multiple aspects of the perceptible were born are deemed to be male. Energy, strength, and the power through which such abstract forms become perceptible realities are female. This is why, in the Hindu pantheon, each aspect of the manifesting being, each god, only has any existence, any reality, any power to manifest itself, when it is united with its female companion or counterpart, its shakti, or power.

The uniting of the phallus and the female organ is the symbol of divine reality, as also of cosmic and physical reality. This union is the origin and end of existence, as well as the cause of its continuation. The sexual act is thus the most important of rites and, accomplished as a rite, is the most effective means of participating in the cosmic work. All other rituals are its image and reproduce this union symbolically. Agni, the god of fire, the male principle, is manifest in the *kunda*, the altar hearth, the female image. The *Upanishads* explain all the aspects of sacrificial ritual as different steps in the act of love.

Woman is the hearth, the male organ is the fire. Caresses are smoke, the vulva is the flame, penetration the firebrand, pleasure the spark. In this fire, the gods sacrifice their seed and a child is born. (*Chandogya Upanishad 5, 4–8*)

The call is the invocation of the deity. The request is the first hymn of praise. Lying beside the woman is the hymn of glory. Lying face to face with her is the choir. The paroxysm is the consecration. Separation is the final hymn. He who knows that this hymn of *Vamadeva* [the god of the left hand, or the Tantric aspect of Shiva] is woven on the act of love procreates himself again with every union. He will live for one hundred years, life's normal length. His progeny and his cattle are numerous. Great is his fame. (*Chandogya Upanishad 2, 13, 1*)

In both Vedic sacrifices and domestic rituals, the wife's presence and participation are indispensable. Woman has an essential sacerdotal function even in public rites and, like the man, must prepare for it by fasting and purification.

When a man renounces the world, his rank, and social duty to devote himself to his spiritual realization, he loses his caste and name, and wears the robe of mourning, the orange colored robe of the monk. In his new condition, caste differences are abolished. This way is also open to women. India's history is full of *yoginis*, female *yogis*, practicing the incredible austerities of saints, wandering the roads from temple to temple, singing the praises of some god.

During the third stage of his life, when the aging man leaves his house and his fortune to his sons and withdraws to the forest to meditate, his wife accompanies him. Later on, the man even renounces his hermitage and has to depart alone, without any human baggage. His wife then returns to her children, or else herself follows the solitary way of the wandering monk.

Woman's nature, like her function, is a double one. All women have two natures, two entirely distinct characters. She is wife and she is mother. As a lover, she represents strength, the creative power of the male principle, which is sterile without her. She is his inspiration, the tool for his realization, the source of his pleasure. She is the image of Shakti, the power and joy of the gods that, without her, have no existence. It is in her role as mother, however, that woman represents the transcendent aspect of the divine. She is the supreme refuge. Here, the male has no role to play. The Mother-Goddess is the sole source of being, the supreme state of consciousness, the principle of life. She is the image of the calm of the primordial night to which man aspires, tossed on the ocean of life and seeking to regain that state of perfection, that total peace from which he came. The Universal Mother thus appears to man as the supreme state of divinity. For him, the Absolute is a female principle. The primordial immensity, the Brahman, the indeterminate substrate, is itself only an unoriented basis. The whole of Creation—all thought, all form, all existence—comes from that mysterious energy that appears in the substrate, from that great matrix that produces forms and beings, the great Goddess, the Universal Mother.

It is thus as mother that woman is the symbol of the transcendent aspect of the divine, as mother that she is divine and is worshipped. A mother is without artifice, she is "without make-up" (*niranjana*). She is the consolation of man, wandering through the deserts of the world. She is forgiveness, charity, limitless compassion. The woman who realizes perfection in her material state is the gate of heaven itself.

THE TEN FORMS OF TRANSCENDENTAL KNOWLEDGE (*MAHA-VIDYA*)[1]

The forms of esoteric knowledge are represented by ten goddesses or female principles presiding over successive aspects of cosmic manifestation. These ten aspects have a cyclical nature and are symbolically associated with the various moments of the day-night cycle. They are known as the Forms of Transcendental Knowledge (*Maha-vidya*) and are the subject of various secret teachings, cults, disciplines, and rituals. The best known of these deities of knowledge is the one associated with the daily cycle at the hour of midnight, representing the principle that presides over the destruction of worlds. This is Kali, the Power of Time that devours all, whose radiant darkness appears more brilliant than a million suns to initiates and to her faithful. Kali is the only door that can lead beyond time, beyond destruction, beyond any form of existence. She is the eternal unconditioned darkness of absolute knowledge, way beyond all light.

In her esoteric form, Kali is the most widely worshipped of Indian goddesses. Her image is frightening. She appears black, hideous, grimacing, her long teeth protruding from her mouth. Her lolling tongue is red. She dances on top of a corpse close to a funeral pyre. She is naked, emaciated, her hair tangled, a necklace of skulls hangs on her withered breasts. Everything about her appearance is horrible, yet her followers sing hymns to her that inspire delirious love, limitless tenderness. This is because she incarnates the great and wonderful mystery of the power of time, which reduces to ruins, to cinders and decay, everything that exists. Nothing can resist her power. Even the gods themselves are her victims. The most divinely beautiful forms are doomed to the horror of decline, decrepitude, to the decay that precedes their disappearance. Yet, beyond this certainty, all religions preach a hope, the hope of a return to a perfect, prenatal state in the generous matrix of time from which all has issued forth.

We cannot attain what is beyond by forgetting decline and death. It is only when we dare to face the reality of our final and total destruction that we begin to perceive what is beyond time. For us, Kali, the Power of Time, is this symbol, this door, this refuge. It is by meditating on the horror of her form, comprising everything we wish to forget, everything that frightens us, that *through* her we can find *in* her true beauty, peace, knowledge of the real beyond all the illusions of transitory forms.

The second form of knowledge is Tara, the devourer, the star that reigns after Kali over the night hours preceding dawn. Tara, "she who leads toward the other bank," represents the power of hunger. In a universe conceived of as perpetual combustion, nothing can exist but by devouring something. Fire devours its fuel, the sun devours its substance, no being can survive without devouring other beings. Tara represents this aptitude to devour, this cosmic hunger, the principle of which necessarily precedes all physical existence.

After Tara, Shodasi appears, the "girl of sixteen," who incarnates all the beauty of created form, the harmony of the spheres. She presides over the exquisite moments of dawn and represents whatever is organized, perfect, wonderful, desirable. Harmony and beauty are the very nature of the visible world that appears to us in its adolescent and perfect form, sixteen years old—the age of the gods—in the splendor of the morning.

After the sixteen-year-old girl comes Bhuvaneshvari, "sovereign of the worlds," who symbolizes the power of knowledge in its fullness, realization of the nature of the cosmos that only exists when it is perceived. This power of knowledge, which reigns over the rich hours before noon, is represented as a goddess in the full force of her femininity, with full breasts and an abundant form. She is the source of revelation of the Veda.

Before midday Chinnamasta, the decapitated one, appears, symbolizing the universe envisaged as a ritual, a sacrifice. All life's deeds, all accomplishments of thought can be envisaged as a sacrificial ritual, as participation in the cosmic sacrifice. To understand the value of the offering of love, the offering of life, the offering of death, we must know the nature of the decapitated one, the eternal sacrificial victim on the altar of the universe. She is associated with the virtue of courage, the bravery of the soldier who gives his life, or of the willing human victim who approaches the altar.

At the hot midday hour, we see Bhairaivi the Terrible appear, representing the power of death. Not the violent end of the sacrifice, but the secret, sweet power of death that begins its insidious work in all beings, in all things, from their very birth. Bhairaivi is beautiful, tender, sensuous. Her sure hand guides us through life's labyrinth and helps us understand the perpetual reality of death.

She is followed by Dhumavati, the Smoky, who represents the condition that follows death, when the destroyed universe is no more than smoke. She is a widow, having reduced the corpse of the world, her husband, to ashes. We see her appear wherever we see the spectacle of poverty, misery, despair. Her yellow, aggressive, fleshless face is that of the beggar, the leper, the abandoned. She delights in deserts, famines, and mourning.

The end of the afternoon is the moment of Bagala, the perfidious, who represents the instinct of destruction, the desire to kill, to destroy every other living being but herself, which is latent in all beings and secretly guides many of our actions. Bagala is the deity of intrigue, magic, poisons, evil spells. She inspires a taste for torture, her pleasure is to see suffering.

In the last gleams of the sunset appears Matangi, the Power of the Elephant, who represents the taste for power and domination. She incarnates royal virtues and dispenses justice. She establishes order and peace, but in actual fact is only a mirage. Shining on her golden throne, she reigns over the night of illusion.

The last of the forms of transcendental knowledge is called Kamala, the Lotus-girl. She protects the world of appearances and is the exact opposite of the Smoky one. She symbolizes splendor, wealth, and is in many ways like Lakshmi, the goddess of fortune and knowledge. Dressed in gold, she is resplendent and beautiful. White elephants incline precious vases toward her, from which heavenly ambrosia flows. The goddess of merchants, she represents the power of wealth, the support of the rites and social peace. She is the source of all stable power and reigns over the early hours of the night.

We can recognize and venerate in woman, in the various forms she takes during her lifetime, or during the cycle of transmigrations, all those aspects of cosmic destiny of which she is the symbol and incarnation. We perceive the goddess in the adolescent, the young woman, the mature and beautiful woman, as well as in the cruel, inhuman woman, the abandoned, emaciated, decrepit woman, the widow, the witch, the beggar, the leper. This is not at all merely an external veneration, but of perceiving in the female body the visible symbols of the nature of cosmic energy, of divine, eternal power, of creative force, of beauty, grandeur, decline, and death.

For the Hindu, every woman is the perceptible expression of the goddess—not merely a human being who symbolizes her—but the mysterious manifestation of those aspects of cosmic power that we must learn to penetrate and understand in order to escape the interminable cycle of illusion that we believe to be life.

To understand the attitude of society and of the Hindu male toward woman, one must always remember her double role as slave and goddess, which makes her a dependent being on one level, but deified and worshipped on the other. To the Hindu, this complex attitude is not at all arbitrary, but expresses the very nature of the female principle. Only Hindu society recognizes and perfects this status that necessarily exists elsewhere in a more or less apparent form, since it is the expression of the inner and inevitable reality of the created world.

The Ahir Caste at Benares

There are few aspects of Indian civilization that have been so wrongly understood and so badly presented as the caste institution. Caste is not merely an economic factor. In general terms, it is the continuation of a people, a particular civilization which, in order to coexist with others, avoids as far as possible any mixed breeding, reciprocal influence, and cultural and social leveling.

In India, three main stocks can be distinguished in population and culture: the Proto-Australoids, related to the Mon-Khmers, speaking Munda languages and practicing animist religions; then peoples of the Gangetic type, who originally spoke Dravidian languages and as a rule still belong to the Shaivite religion; and lastly, the "Aryan," or Aryanized, peoples, speaking Indo-Aryan languages, whose religion is derived from the Vedas. At a time that we now consider historic, Jainism, the ancient ethical and atheistic religion of the Dravidians, was reintegrated into the Hindu family, followed by the return of Buddhism, which was initially a reaction against ritual excesses. Much later, we see the Sikh religion appear, which is a Hindu adaptation of the Islamic message. Lastly, in our own times, owing to the importation of Christianity after conquest by the West, we see the development of Arya Samaj, Brahmo Samaj, and, above all, the order of Ramakrishna, which are Hindu adaptations of the Christian message. Europe has quite naturally been in contact with these new religious branches and has tended to exaggerate their importance, especially the fact that they express themselves in Western languages, which orthodox Hinduism refuses to do.

The ancient Jewish, Christian, and Parsi communities who took refuge in India, as well as the autochthonous religious groups, such as Buddhists, Jains, and Sikhs, have never met with persecution. The same can be said of the primitive peoples, still living in the Stone Age, who have been miraculously protected. The attitude of later invaders, first Muslims, then Christians, has been very different. Their missionary spirit is in total contrast with the freedom of speech, customs, and way of life that the caste institution has sought to preserve. Their so-called egalitarianism only exists to the extent that the conquered peoples adopt their way of life, religion, and habits. Groups that have been persecuted elsewhere are very conscious of this, and only demand freedom to be themselves. The important castes—which are not necessarily the ones known as the "high castes"—have as a rule largely maintained their social institutions, customs, religion, and sometimes even their language, history, traditional oral literature, music, dances, festivals, and so on, which in some cases are a direct continuation from prehistoric times. Current affairs are managed by a council of five notables (the panchayat), without any intervention by the state or by individuals belonging to other communities.

One interesting example is that of the Ahirs, the descendents of an ancient and very independent people, the Abhiras, who nowadays form a highly respected Shudra caste, and whose profession is the raising of cattle and milk production. They are a dark-skinned caste of the ancient Gangetic type, having no apparent ethnic connection with the Proto-Australoids or with Aryanized elements. They have kept the beliefs, ways of life, and traditions of the ancient pre-Aryan Shaivite culture. In all probability, they belong to the highly civilized people that settled on the Indian sub-continent during the second millennium B.C.E., who were enemies of the Vedic Aryans. Today they still form an important part of the population of southern India, and numerous groups are scattered throughout Orissa, the Himalayan regions, central India, and elsewhere.

AHIR LANGUAGE AND TRADITIONS

From a cultural point of view, the Ahirs belong to the same culture as the dark-skinned heroes of the *Ramayana* and the *Mahabharata*, Rama and Krishna, referred to by their important orally-transmitted "historical texts." Krishna, the hero of the *Mahabharata*, was raised in this community. His love affairs with the cowgirls of Brindavana are famous. Part of the Tamil novel *Shilappadikaram*,[1] dating roughly from the third century C.E., is set in an Ahir village, where the customs are practically the same as in Ahir villages in northern India today. Nowadays, the Ahirs of Benares speak a Hindi dialect that is different from the one used by other castes. Like most popular languages of northern India, its grammatical forms and expressions indicate the existence of an original Dravidian substrate. Their customs, social laws, and rules concerning property and inheritance differ from those of other castes. Polyandry and matriarchy are no longer found, but repudiation and divorce remain easy. Their festivals are peculiar to them and their religion belongs entirely to ancient Shaivism, featuring the phallus cult. It should be noted that, contrary to what is often believed, the lewd festivals, songs, and dances do not imply orgiastic customs or freedom of morals.

Although these peoples are not warriors, they attach great importance to physical exercise and male strength. The women do not take part in the men's songs and dances. They have their own dances, which are relatively static and are totally different from those of the men. The women's dances are held on the enormous beaten-earth courtyards of their houses, which persons outside the group may not attend. They are accompanied exclusively by songs and the clapping of hands. The songs as a rule are in praise of the girls' beauty, assurances of success with a handsome youth, and invocations to the goddess.

BARDS AND DRUM PLAYERS

The community's bards preserve its traditional oral literature in the form of chanted narratives. There is a considerable amount of this oral literature. Some elements are common to the Shaivite *Puranas*. These *Puranas* or oral "ancient chronicles" of the Ahirs comprise numerous narratives referring to forgotten wars, towns that disappeared centuries ago, and events of all kinds of which there is no trace in official histories. These accounts are of great interest, but no effort has been made to transcribe them. At the same time, the poet-musicians continually add to these ancient narratives new chants referring to contemporary events, whose style in no way differs from the former. In the Brailoiu Universal Collection, I published a recording of a very archaic type of Ahir chant, whose text referred to the bombing of the Benares railway bridge by the Japanese in 1942.

Bards and drum players do not form a special group within the caste. They have the same profession as the others, and any boy can learn to chant their oral literature. For practical reasons, however, there is a certain tendency for a bard to teach his repertory to his son, or to a boy he has more or less adopted. Bards are held in high esteem. They rank among the notables of the caste, and their most important member is almost inevitably one of the panchayat that settles all internal problems. He is a kind of "man-of-letters," who must formerly have played some sort of sacerdotal role and may do so even now. The drum players, on the other hand, are neither looked down upon, nor particularly esteemed. Neither bards nor musicians are paid. Money plays no role in the group's internal relations, and serves only for external needs.

EROTIC DANCES AND MUSIC

The Ahirs' dances are extremely erotic, comprising a dance performed by young men—one of whom is dressed as a woman—who mime scenes of love and copulation. The accompaniment is dominated by drums (large and small kettle drums) whose noise is deafening. The music, consisting of songs, is mingled with obscene remarks, accompanied only by the drums. Some Ahirs know how to play the flute, but wind or string instruments are never employed for dances. It would be considered a kind of sacrilege. This notion is found among many archaic groups in India, where music is essentially formed of songs and drums. Other instruments are intruders, modern things, never allowed in the rites. The erotic dance has maintained its fundamentally magical and ritual nature, which is to ward off ill-omened influences and evil spirits and create a kind of safe area for the participants.

At the Spring festival (Holi), young Ahirs, together with young men from other similar castes, process with wooden phalluses painted red, performing suggestive dances, making obscene remarks, and preceded by a man dressed as Shiva (his body painted white, wearing a long black wig), bearing a trident and mounted on an ass or, if an ass is not available, on a horse.

The Ahirs' music has no common characteristic with the music of other communities in northern India. The *raga* system has not influenced it in the slightest. Their style of singing, drum technique, scales, and intervals all belong to a family quite different from the habitual music of northern India. Some musical forms are, however, related to those of certain communities in southern India and in several Himalayan regions. This is certainly one of the most ancient musical languages of India, and a highly detailed investigation would be needed to establish its relations with the innumerable separate Shaivite communities scattered all over the Indian continent.

Such an investigation is especially difficult since communities with different traditions coexist in the same places, as at Benares and in other regions. In Kumaon (Almora), the music of the ancient Shaivite populations—now considered low caste, although they still have their own priests and princes—is close to that of the Ahirs and has nothing in common with the folklore of the Brahmans and the groups of the population with which they are associated.

On the Work of Abbé Dubois:

Customs, Institutions, and Ceremonies of the Peoples of India

THE PERSON

Born in 1765, Jean Antoine Dubois was ordained just prior to the French Revolution. Fearing the violence of the revolutionaries against religious orders and believing that his life was in danger, he decided to leave for India as a missionary. It appears that he was given no previous training to give him some idea about the culture and customs of the land to which he was to bring what was for him the message of the true faith.

This lack of preparation partly explains the naïveté of his observations, a curious mixture of horror and admiration, of good will and incongruity, that characterizes his description of the manners and customs of southern India, where he lived uninterruptedly for thirty years.

His ministry was to look after Christianized Indians who were, almost without exception, Shudras (members of the artisan castes), or Pariahs (castes practicing contaminating professions, such as cesspool clearers, cobblers, leather workers, and so on). He consequently approached Indian civilization starting from the lowest level of society, and its customs and beliefs, unlike modern people, who are first and foremost interested in the highest forms of culture and spiritual life.

The observations and reactions of Abbé Dubois may therefore appear somewhat surprising.

His linguistic knowledge was apparently limited to everyday Tamil. He was probably unable to read literary or philosophical works, but he did learn the Tamil alphabet and mentions several low-caste satirical authors. What he knew of Sanskrit literature and of the Hindus' sacred books was limited to information gleaned from the village Brahmans, in the Tamil tongue. His transcriptions of words, done by ear, often makes them difficult to recognize, such as "bassouva" for *vrishbha* (bull); "sorna" for *suvarna* (gold); "marou-jemma" for *marana-janma* (metempsychosis); "Ganiza" for Ganesh; "brahmanes cheivas" for Shaivite priests (Shudras); "ezour-védam" for *Yajur Veda*, and so on.

POLITICAL CONDITIONS

Abbé Dubois reached India in 1790, at a time when the Muslim Empire was breaking up. The French had been defeated by the English who, after acquiring sovereignty over Bengal in 1765, were extending their dominion throughout India. Tipu Sultan—the powerful Muslim prince who reigned over Mysore and sought an alliance with the French—had been defeated by the army of Lord Arthur Wellesley and was killed at the battle of Seringapatam in 1799. Shah Alam II, the last titular emperor, was to die in 1806. The Punjab would not be annexed until 1849, and Ranjeet Singh, the powerful Sikh warlord, did not die until 1839. In 1825—the year in which Abbé Dubois's work was published in French—the English annexed Sind and, during the following years, imposed their administration on most of the minor states. The Maratha Confederacy broke down in 1818 and the Rajput princes signed treaties placing them under British tutelage.

Dubois thus found himself in a country that, having been subject to Muslim domination, was now passing under British control. He does not hide his admiration for British administration, which, he says, brought Christian justice and civilization to peoples still living under paganism.

On the recommendation of Major Mark Wilks, the British Resident at Mysore in 1806, Abbé Dubois's manuscript was submitted to Lord William Bentinck, Governor of Madras, and was purchased by the East India Company. It was translated into English and published in London in 1816.

The opinions of Abbé Dubois, being those of a foreigner, were considered impartial, and contributed quite innocently to the British policy of the time, which was the systematic denigration of Hinduism and an attempt at Christianizing the country, a policy that would only be reversed under Queen Victoria, after the Mutiny of 1857–1859.

THE EUROPEANS

The first missionaries—Jesuits as a rule—had come to India in the seventeenth century and had made every effort to learn about the habits and prejudices of the populations so as not to give inadvertent offense. Some of them called themselves Roman Brahmans and, at least in appearance, observed the rules of life of the Indian religious. They avoided eating meat and drinking alcohol, entering houses without taking off their shoes, and touching people. They also performed ablutions and—quite clearly—avoided taking any interest in women. They consequently acquired a certain prestige and made a considerable number of converts. This method was to be copied in the twentieth century by other missionaries, such as Père Monchanin.

With the arrival of European soldiers and officials, things changed completely. Their customs and manners filled the Hindus with horror, disgust, and contempt, even among the humblest, including the neo-Christians. Abbé Dubois, aware of this fact, does not spare his criticisms of the Europeans, the more so since—for him—Christianity was the goal of colonization and both officials and soldiers were its wretched messengers.

"The Brahman does not believe in his religion, but he practices it; the Christian believes in his, but does not practice it." Owing to their habits, Europeans could only employ as servants unscrupulous Pariahs, which isolated them from the body of Hindu society, including the artisan masses.

THE METHOD

Abbé Dubois can be considered as one of the first practitioners of a method that was later to obtain its "scientific" patent under the name of ethnology. In short, he settled in the midst of a people whose language he did not speak, whose history and religion he did not know, and set himself to describe their habits, rites, customs, and beliefs, either from his own observations or from what his interlocutors told him.

Such a method has its drawbacks. First, there are the observer's own convictions and customs, causing him to make judgments about what he considers barbarous, irrational, disgusting, unjust, inhuman, or ridiculous. Dubois expresses his opinions with remarkable violence. What is interesting about his investigation—as well as being its weak point—is that he lived in the most underprivileged surroundings, that of the lowest castes, to which almost all his Christians belonged. He had very few contacts with the other social classes, about which he makes uninformed and rather caricature-like judgments.

For him, the Shudras (the artisan classes), forming the fourth level of the social ladder, are "the most respectable and most interesting class, which directs public opinion and keeps proper order in society." This point of view is not entirely fallacious, but for reasons he appears not to understand, such as the origin of the different population groups. The artisans are, in actual fact, the autochthonous Dravidians, whereas the Brahmans are foreigners, Aryans, who came from the north. His assertion of the superiority of the people as compared to the establishment is rather surprising, coming from a man who had fled the Revolution and considered it with horror.

THE BIBLE

Apart from a few scraps from Latin authors, the Abbé's cultural background largely consisted of the Bible. "I had no other reading matter but my Bible." This often led him to make comparisons—which are not without interest—between the customs of the Hebrews and those of the

Hindus. He notes similarities in their purification and birth rites, the unclean period for women, their sacrifices. He compares the versions of the flood whose date, for him, is of course that of the Bible. From his point of view, the seven penitents (*rishis*), who escaped from the catastrophe of the flood, whom he considers as the forefathers of the Brahman dynasties, can be none other than the seven sons of Japhet. In the same way, Gautama is Magog, Brahma is Prometheus, and so on.

THE CASTES

The Abbé's attitude toward the castes is worthy of note, because he sees this institution from the point of view of the humble and not—following the rule—from that of the more favored groups.

He expresses his admiration for a social system based on the corporation, a sort of extended family, which assures each group, even the most humble, its autonomy, religious, and institutional freedom, along with the right to survive and to maintain its genetic and cultural heritage, of which it is proud. He emphasizes the "superiority of the ties of caste over those of the family" in protecting the individual. Dubois considers that the caste system is "a masterpiece of Indian legislation," since it "unites both religious and political [aspects]." He deems that "without the castes, the people would fall into barbarianism and anarchy." "The caste is a powerful part of social order." "I do not believe," he says, "that the idea of abolishing the castes would ever be entertained by a reasonable person." "The ignominy that is shared by a whole tribe for the faults of one person, if they remain unpunished, force the tribe itself to do justice to avenge its honor and to keep its members within the bounds of duty."

Here he shares the point of view of orthodox Hinduism that I have explained in my book *Virtue, Success, Pleasure, and Liberation: Traditional India's Social Structures, The Four Aims of Life in the Tradition of Ancient India*.

The theoretical abolition of the castes carried out by the government of modern India, steeped in imported socialistic ideas, could only lead, according to Abbé Dubois, to political error. According to the principle he emphasizes, the Sikh community is responsible for settling the fate of a few fanatical terrorists. Dubois is not against a certain very moderate form of slavery practiced in India. He compares the advantages of the Malabar Pariah slaves, who are part of the family to whom they belong, eat the same food as their masters and have a life without problems, with the wretchedness of the free Pariahs, and particularly the Christian ones. In actual fact, he poses the problem of guaranteed employment, which, in any society, entails the loss of certain liberties.

Dubois distinguishes the Shudras, often rich and prosperous, from the Pariahs and outcastes, a distinction that is often neglected in modern descriptions of Hindu society.

Dubois's attitude toward the Brahmans is the same as that of a man of the people toward the lower clergy. He clearly knew only the village priests and never had access to any great scholars. At the same time, the gluttony of ignorant priests is a comic theme that is often exploited in classical Sanskrit plays. Even in Europe, there are thousands of tales, more or less obscene, about the lewdness and craftiness of monks, although this is merely a very marginal aspect of reality. The Church's value cannot be estimated through the *Decameron*.

Dubois's violent attacks above all reflect the hostility of the Dravidians toward the Aryan Brahmans who came from the north, a hostility that in our own times has given rise to a political anti-Brahman movement in southern India.

For Dubois, "the Brahmans are by nature crafty, slippery, double-dealing, groveling. They know how to profit by their unpraiseworthy qualities. . . . Brahmans are better educated, more crafty and more slippery than other Indians. They have become necessary even to the Muslim princes, who cannot do without them for administrative details. . . . They have also been clever enough to worm their way into the confidence of the great European power that nowadays dominates India."

Dubois does, however, know about the existence of non-Brahman Shaivite priests. He mentions the "Vallouvers," who are the "Brahmans of the Pariahs." The origin of these priestly dynasties going back to pre-

Aryan Shaivism is explained in my book *While the Gods Play, Shaiva Oracles and Predictions on the Cycle of History and the Destiny of Mankind*.[1]

MARRIAGE AND POPULATION

Dubois considers that the impoverishment of India, whose riches had formerly astounded the whole world, was due to population increase. Under ancient Hindu law, any such increase was limited by two main factors: the prohibition of divorce and remarriage of widows, as well as the recommendation for a man who had begotten a son—and thus assured the continuation of his ancestors' line—to devote himself to the chaste life of a Sannyasi (wandering monk).

He spends much time on "the ancient and atrocious custom that makes it a duty for widows to immolate themselves on their husband's funeral pyre" and criticizes the British administration for tolerating it. This practice, already "forbidden by the Muslim princes," was to be legally abolished by Lord Bentinck in 1829, at the request of the religious reformer Rajah Ram Mohan Roy (1774–1833), the founder of the Brahmo Samaj and contemporary of Dubois. The latter, however, apparently had no notion of the great reform movements that were sweeping northern India at that time.

Dubois becomes indignant over this practice, which was also shared by other ancient peoples. Nowadays, people prefer the pill, sterilization, abortion, and killing the fetus, which the Hindus on their side look upon with horror.

It is important, however, to understand the attitude and mentality of the peoples who practice this kind of sacrifice. For the Hindus, human life is but a transitory moment, and fidelity—taken even as far as martyrdom—is an opening on to a future life of heavenly bliss. Women who accept such a heroic sacrifice are saints. The famous Tamil novel, *Manimekhalai*,[2] speaks of it as a sublime deed. The Christians, too, venerate their martyrs. When a captain launches his soldiers, trembling with fear, to the attack, to certain death, they are glorified as heroes. The partisan who breaks down and weeps for fear of being shot is treated as a coward. Laws seeking to forbid such sacrifices depend on the religious and moral concepts of governments, but if we wish to understand the civilization that practices them, we must at least recognize their greatness. It must also be remembered that hundreds of women—the wives of Rajput warriors—threw themselves into the flames rather than fall into the hands of the Muslims.

PHILOSOPHICAL SYSTEMS

The account Dubois gives of the philosophical systems of India is worthy of a stage comedian who, in his indignation, mixes up the most different doctrines. His description of Buddhism, which he calls Baoudah-mata, would certainly surprise its followers.

> According to this odious system, there is no god other than matter.
> . . . There are neither vices nor virtues, neither heaven nor hell. . . .
> The true Buddhist . . . knows no other god than his body . . . and obtains for it all the pleasures of the senses . . . he eats anything, indifferently . . . he knows no god other than himself. . . . It is not surprising that the monsters who profess such odious principles, so contrary to the good of society, have become the object of public execration and have been almost entirely exterminated in India.

On the other hand, Dubois shows a certain esteem for Jainism (an ethical and atheistic religion), which he deems to be the most ancient religion of India and whose extreme puritanism he appreciates. Jains are also still numerous in the south, particularly in Karnataka country, whereas hardly any Buddhists are to be found in that area.

THE TEXTS

Dubois only knows the sacred texts of India by hearsay, as explained to him either in Tamil or in English. His references to certain texts of a practical kind, such as those concerning domestic rites (*Nitya-Karma*) are relatively exact, but the Abbé's ignorance of the rest is remarkable: "The Indians have several books dealing with this magical nonsense. The main one is called *Adarva (Atharva) vedam*. . . . It should not be imagined that these Vedas contain matters of interest . . . the most pitiful fables . . . the metaphors of Vishnu, the infamous lingam, etc."

Clearly, he does not know that the Vedas mention neither the lingam nor the incarnations of Vishnu. At the same time, he is confusing the *Bhagavata Purana*, the great work dealing with the life of Krishna, with the *Bhagavad Gita*, which is merely a chapter of the *Mahabharata*. He is equally ignorant of profane literature. "I do not know," he says, "whether they have real dramatic works." The editor adds: "Only a few plays are worth keeping. The best would be unbearable in Europe."

At the same time, Dubois transcribes with a certain fidelity some of the fables and proverbs of the *Nyaya*. For him, "the *Pancha Tantra*, a collection of fables, is the only text in Indian literature that is instructive and worthy of attention."

As historical works, he mentions the *Ramayana*, the *Bhagavata* and the *Mahabharata*, but regrets that "all the events are as it were buried in a dark abyss of pitiful tales."

ARTS AND CULTURE

The Abbé sets little store by the great temples of southern India, whose existence he hardly mentions. For him, they are "public monuments covered with the filthiest obscenities." As far as painting is concerned, he sees only daubs. He has clearly never heard of Mogul miniatures, nor noticed the admirable icons painted on wood that decorate all the houses of the region in which he lived.

With regard to music, "although the Indians delight in listening to it . . . the sounds they require from their musicians are not harmonious . . . they want sharp and piercing sounds . . . the most insipid monotony reigns over their songs. . . . The vounei [vina], played by Brahmans, makes fairly agreeable sounds however." Yet Dubois was the contemporary of famous musicians such as Shyama Shastri, Tyagaraja, and Dikshitar, who are the glory of Dravidian music.

Dubois does, however, mention the extraordinary refinement of Indian textiles, the manufacture of which occupied a large number of craft workers, which are famous throughout the world (cashmere, madras, and so on). They were systematically ruined by the development of the European textile industry.

For Dubois, "India has no public education system," which is contradicted by the editor's note saying, "India possesses magnificent schools. Many Indian princes have founded and endowed great colleges."

CONCLUSION

Before the beginning of the twentieth century, there were practically no documents on the life, customs, and beliefs of the Indian masses. The Abbé Dubois's book is thus a unique document of great importance. It is the testimony of a man who, at the start of the nineteenth century, lived in close contact with the masses, the low castes, the untouchables, and explains their customs, beliefs, prejudices, virtues, and vices.

Orientalists and linguists who, since the close of the eighteenth century, have taken an interest in Indian civilization, have above all dealt with ancient texts, philosophy, and Vedic religion. Anquetil Duperron (1731–1805) published a translation of several of the *Upanishad*s in 1804. In 1813, H. H. Wilson (1786–1860) published a translation of the *Meghaduta* and, in 1819, his Sanskrit dictionary. His translation of the *Vishnu Purana* appeared in 1840. Burnouf (1801–1852) translated the *Bhagavata Purana*, which was published in 1842–1847. A little later on, several great scholars devoted themselves to studying the civilization of India, such as Max Muller (1823–1900), Paul Deussen (1845–1919), Hermann Jacobi (1850), Max Weber (1853–1892), Hendrik Kern (1865–1903). They were followed by René Guénon, John Woodroffe, Sylvain Levi, Helmuth von Glasenapp, M. Emile Senart, Louis Renou, Jean Filliozat, and others. Their works help us to appreciate the values of a civilization of which the good Abbé was often able to see only the negative aspects.

Traditional society in India has changed little since the beginning of the nineteenth century. I, too, have lived in this society for nearly as long as Abbé Dubois, but my experience of India has been profoundly different, since I approached the matters he mentions from the point of view of a person desirous of learning and refusing to judge.

The recently developed myth of a mystical India, impregnated with religious fervor, often hides from us the real India—that ninety percent of the population is made up of artisans and peasants. In order to understand the political, social, and human problems facing modern India, it is essential to get to know the India of the masses, deepest India, the real India, of which Abbé Dubois provides such a gripping picture at the outset of British colonization. His work will be very useful to modern Indians and foreigners in helping them to understand better certain recent developments in India's history, so long as they do not give too much importance to his judgments, biased by the prejudices of a missionary convinced of Western superiority and the importance of the West's role in spreading the Christian message.

Dubois does not dissimulate his goal, but explains, "In tracing a faithful picture of the turpitude and extravagance of polytheism and idolatry, I feel that its ugliness will highlight the perfection of Christianity to immense advantage."

> God forbid that I should here insult the misfortune of a nation which, plunged into the darkness of idolatry and ignorance, is incapable of escaping by its own means from the gross errors and superstitions that are its consequence. . . . Just so were our own forefathers, just so we would still be ourselves without . . . the revelation and divine light of faith.

The purely objective approach to the ethics and customs of the inhabitants of a village, of whose historical and religious context one is ignorant, as in Dubois's case—which we may term "ethnological"—however important and useful it may be, can sometimes serve as an excuse for a highly pernicious form of colonialism. It is not at all by chance that this book received the approval of the British Residents and was first published in London.

All civilizations possess some debatable aspects, injustices, and cruelties that if exaggerated will suffice to disparage a people and its culture. Christian missionaries have often innocently played this role to the advantage of colonial powers. "Give a dog a bad name and hang it," says the English proverb. Certain modern sects utilize this method for recruitment purposes. Marxist ethnologists too sometimes play a similar role in favor of Soviet expansion, often in complete innocence.

Our interest in testimony like that of Abbé Dubois is very different from the interest that originally led to its publication. What is important nowadays is the information he presents, with undeniable sincerity, about little-known aspects of Indian life at the outset of the nineteenth century.

Evolution and Freedom

Judging from his article in the *Express* (27 December–2 January 1977), Professor Jacques Ruffié is dangerously mixing precise notions with the romantic slogans of our time. He shows us an evolutionary tree with its increasing differentiation of species and then, suddenly, he would have us believe that "having pushed to their extreme limit the possibilities of the independent organism . . . it remains for man to make a final synthesis by grouping together individual consciousness in a single society in which ethics replace instinct[!]," which would be a "mixture of whites, blacks, and yellows" because "crossbreeding is part of the fundamental behavior of living beings." The example given of the birch moth does not imply that the moth adapts itself but that, according to the color of the environment, the black ones or the white ones have the best advantage, *while the others are exterminated*. That has nothing to do with crossbreeding.

Promoting "a world without races or frontiers" means confusing the fundamental reality of evolution with artificial territorial divisions. No reasoning can be based on such arguments. Why should one want to eliminate the highly diverse beauty of species and bastardize them?

One of the tragedies of our time is the systematic destruction of human races that cannot adapt to the so-called "modern" world, in which they are exterminated to give the illusion of an egalitarian world.

One should ask the Pygmies, the Australian Aborigines, the tribes of India, what they think about it. Crossbreeding them to make them sub-white will always serve some purpose, but is that Professor Ruffié's goal, or is he dreaming?

India has long taught us that respect for different races is the key to coexistence. Certain kinds of antiracism are the opposite of respect for human species. Hybridization is merely a hypocritical and totally racist solution, which is certainly not part of the natural evolutionary plan.

The opposite of "racism" is the protection of minorities. This is not egalitarianism, which, being utopian, is in practice an easy way of camouflaging genocide. Creating a single human species by mixing all the races goes against the very principle of evolution itself, and means suppressing the problem rather than solving it.

"Leveling is, in all things, death," as Hindu philosophy tells us.

The Dictatorship of the Pen-Pushers, or *Alpha-Bêtise-Me* *

LANGUAGE

All animals have a language, a visual, auditory, olfactory, and tactile tool of expression and communication, comprising sounds, signs, smells, and mime. Bees have a dancing language. We know nothing about the wave transmission of insects, since we ourselves possess no developed emitting and receiving organs, although they exist in us as a potential, as shown by accidental long-distance perception and thought reading, faculties that can be developed by yoga techniques. The fundamental difference between humans and other living species appears to be the development of an elaborate spoken language. Visual language has seen a great step forward in our own times and will certainly have a profound influence on the organization of our mental faculties.

Among human species, there are several major families of spoken languages, each of which has developed a vocabulary and structures

---

*Translator's Note: In the title of this essay, the author is making a pun on *Alphabétisme*, using the second half of the word as *bêtise*, meaning "stupidity," which is impossible to convey in English.

73

that appear to have nothing in common, although mutual borrowings throughout their long history sometimes make such delimitations difficult.

All existing languages, as well as their content, the relationship of their sounds and ideas, were formulated and structured over many millennia through oral tradition. A language is defined by its vocabulary, based on key sounds—roots—as well as by its grammar, or art of word assembly. It appears that new roots or word-assembly procedures are never invented. India's grammarians deem that all languages were originally monosyllabic, tone languages, like Chinese and Vietnamese. English has preserved a considerable vocabulary coming from a prehistoric monosyllabic tongue, which makes it a particularly creative language. From the same source come the names of most of our rivers, as well as certain place names.

CULTURE AND WRITING

The culture of any human group is made up of an accumulation of knowledge and ideas formulated and transmitted by the intermediary of a particular language—utilizing a certain number of symbols, words, that do not always have equivalents in other languages—which as a whole forms the originality, the contribution of a culture to the species' heritage of knowledge. Thus, over the millennia, a collective memory came into being, including a vast body of data that forms the substratum of all cultures. This knowledge, recorded in our memory, is transmitted together with the language itself, from parent to child or from teacher to pupil.

The Oral Tradition

In all regions of the world, language was formed and a heritage of philosophic, religious, mythical, historical, and literary vocabulary constituted by means of oral tradition. Even today, most of humanity's cultural heritage is transmitted orally. In India, besides the epic and historical texts, transcribed at a relatively recent period, there are still epic poems and historical accounts that are transmitted solely by oral tradition, thanks to folk singers. In Africa, almost all cultural heritage exists only in the form of oral tradition.

In countries where writing now plays a predominant role, there appears to be little awareness of the part played by oral tradition, teaching, words, and discourse in transmitting the fundamental elements of culture. However, the rudiments of language are not learned through writing. Only when the child possesses all the elements of language, the bases of vocabulary and grammatical structures that impact thought, does he begin to read. This stage is never reached by most of humankind and even by many people in literate countries. Illiterates are not less capable of expressing themselves, reflecting, or practicing all kinds of professions that require a high level of intelligence and knowledge. In our schools, even when written textbooks are used, teaching is always oral and remains an essential aspect of knowledge transmission. Politicians always make their mark in speeches and debates rather than in written messages. Professorial teaching is still a basic fact in universities.

For a large section of humankind, cultural transmission is still ensured by "living books"—bards and masters—whose social function is to spread and transmit the group's cultural heritage. Their highly trained memory allows bards and priests to have at their fingertips a considerable amount of cultural information, which they then adapt to particular needs. Mnemonic techniques have been developed to ensure the continuity and permanence of knowledge. Other procedures are used to establish, accumulate, diffuse, and transmit the language's sound symbols, the body of knowledge that makes up oral tradition, through the vehicle of words.

Chanted versification is one of the means utilized to ensure the memorization and transmission of knowledge. It is one of the most effective techniques for transmitting scientific or philosophical knowledge, discoveries, laws, and myths. This was the method used to constitute the Vedas, the Bible, the Homeric poems, the Upanishads, and innumerable legendary accounts, maxims, and proverbs, summarizing cultural observations, reflections, and knowledge acquired over centuries or millennia, before they were ever transcribed.

In India, the precise transmission of the verified sacred texts, the

Vedas, is assured by utilizing special techniques. Brahman boys learn them by heart according to patterns, that is, the syllables of each verse are memorized both forward and backward, jumping one syllable in two, one in three, and so on, according to a purely mechanical process guaranteeing permanence and transmission, even by those who do not understand the meaning. Philosophical and religious texts, such as the Upanishads, are also in highly condensed verse form.

In the same way, children learn versified forms of the definitions of the Sanskrit dictionary (*Amar Kosha*), as well as treatises on astronomy, mathematics, mythology, genealogy, and history. We know that verse formulas are easier to memorize than prose texts. Even in the modern West, children still learn poems by heart.

To ensure the continued existence of texts, the defenders of knowledge in India, during the second half of the first millennium B.C.E., created an artificial language—Sanskrit (the "refined language")—for the use of scholars, theologians, and philosophers. This fixed language, which does not develop, is an ideal tool for storing knowledge. For this purpose, they utilized the basic structures and roots of the Vedic language, enriched with numerous elements coming from pre-Aryan tongues. Some specialists consider that the first Sanskrit grammar belongs to the oral tradition and was only transcribed much later on. This scholarly language was not intended to replace the popular languages, which are constantly evolving, each bringing a different contribution to the modulations of thought and knowledge. Sanskrit is and remains a scholars' language.

Writing

Although signs have been engraved on shells, stone, or clay since prehistoric times to indicate ownership, kind, or number, writing that could note or transcribe sentences or texts appears as a relatively recent phenomenon in the history of humankind. Indeed, it only involves certain civilizations. In various forms, writing appeared as a simultaneous discovery in China, India, Mesopotamia, and Egypt, in about the third millennium B.C.E. For a long time, it was used for transmitting messages, establishing accounts, recording the names of the dead, invoking deities, and sometimes for noting down legendary events, for the purpose of remembering them, but it never interfered with the oral transmission of knowledge of the sciences and arts.

Such writing only concerned priests, scholars, and—to a certain extent—merchants. It was never very widespread and vanished in many regions as a result of barbarian invasions. This was what happened to the ancient Cretan language during the Dorian invasion and, in the Middle East, with the arrival of the "sea-people." In India, the Aryan invasion almost totally eliminated the writing inherited from the Indus Valley civilization. These early forms of writing had made it possible to fix a considerable amount of knowledge till then transmitted by oral tradition, which reappeared once writing had vanished.

Only in a few cases, at Sumer and in Egypt, were some of these early texts miraculously preserved, to be rediscovered after several thousands of years. These ancient traditions of writing of a syllabic or ideographical kind survived only in a more or less fragmentary fashion in protected areas or in hidden form. Their traces and influence can be encountered here and there in later writing. Their marks are mostly a kind of mnemonic technique, rather than any attempt to transcribe the language phonetically.

Only toward the eighth century B.C.E. was a new form of consonantal writing invented by the Phoenicians, which spread rapidly throughout the Mediterranean world, the Middle East, Persia, and India.

In China, although the hexagrams used by magicians for divining purposes date from the twelfth century, it was only in the third century B.C.E. that—thanks to the discovery of ink and the paintbrush—Chinese writing developed. Modern Chinese writing dates from the third century C.E., and it is only in our own times that the ancient ideograms have begun to be threatened by phonetic writing of Phoenician origin.

The Vedic texts and their annexes, which have played a fundamental role in Indian culture starting from the second millennium B.C.E., were only transcribed starting from the fifth century B.C.E., with the importation of Aramaic writing by the Persians.

It was only at a very recent period that any attempt was made to establish a written body of knowledge, an attempt that at the same time tends to oppose the oral tradition. Writing means that certain texts can be fixed and transmitted, but this is not always an advantage because it leads to the destruction of the collective memory and in any case only concerns selected texts. Writing makes it easy for texts to be falsified, or used dogmatically, placing those who "know the secret" in an unjustifiable position of power. The discovery, by some human groups, of methods of preserving certain elements of language in the form of writing gave them considerable power over other groups who, for the accumulation of their cultural data, utilized only the vast reservoir of memory, from which knowledge can be solely transmitted by oral tradition.

Writing is a marvelous tool for storing certain forms of knowledge, certain creations of the human spirit at a given period. However, the tool of thought, of the transmission of knowledge, is still the spoken language. Philosophers and scholars reflect and seek to formulate their thoughts through language symbols (which they have learned through the oral tradition) before they transcribe them. The spoken language and its reflection—the written language—must not be confused. Like painting and sculpture, which are much earlier, writing was originally a means of communication through time and space. It is a method for preserving certain knowledge for the use of future generations. It allows us to preserve a picture of some of the elements of knowledge of a given period. It is only secondarily a means for immediate communication. Even in the West, most working class people can only write stereotyped formulas on postcards.

Language, which is a tool for formulating and transmitting thought, is only effective if we possess all the necessary elements in our memory. Clearly, some elements can be understood when written down, but the subtleties, the humor and the nuances of language can only be appreciated in its oral or spoken form, which cannot be acquired from writing. That is why the teaching of language by pen-pushers in schools—in speaking of writing—is only interesting in the case of dead languages and never widens our possibility of expression, of adding new elements to the formulation of our thought.

MEMORIZATION AND DOCUMENTATION

The memorization process is an important part of knowledge, even in cultures in which writing now plays a major part. We store a considerable number of formulas, words, and poems, forming a mental treasury on which we draw constantly. The rhythmic or metric form is an important aid to memory.

I have long ago forgotten the geometrical theorems I studied in my childhood, but some of them, expressed in rhyme, are still immediately accessible, such as:

> *Le volume de la sphère*
> *Est égal, quoi qu'on puisse faire,*
> *Aux quat'tiers de Pi R 3*
> *Même si la sphère est en bois*
> *Le polygone convexe*
> *N'a qu'une chose qui le vexe*
> *C'est d'être toujours plus petit*
> *Que son confrère circonscrit.*
> *Le carré de l'hypoténuse*
> *est égal, si je ne m'abuse*
> *A la somme des carrés*
> *Construits sur les aut'côtés.*

It is thanks to the same method that I have constantly at my fingertips the concise texts of the Upanishads, which I use to support my reflections on the nature of the world, such as the *Isha Upanishad*:

> *Ishavashyam idam sarvam*
> *Yatkincha jagatyam jagat*
> *Tena tyaktena bhunjitha*
> *Ma Ghridha Kasyasvid dhanam*

> *In a world where everything changes [where nothing is permanent] the divine is everywhere present [in flowers, birds, animals, in forests, in man].*

Enjoy fully what the god concedes to you and never covet what belongs to others [neither their goods, nor their talent, nor their success].

Similarly, my mind still remembers the *Bhagavad Gita*:

Dharma Kshetre Kuru Kshetre samaveta yuyutsavah Mamaka Pandavaschaiva, Kim Akurvante, Samjaya! . . .

On the "field of justice," the plain of the northern invaders, where they have gathered, ready to fight, tell me, Samjaya, what my people and those of the Pandavas are doing . . .

Even though it was transmitted at a certain time in writing, this inner thesaurus has quite a different value from what I own in the form of books on the shelves of my library. It only comes to life again for use in creative thought when it has been rerecorded in my memory and has returned to the oral tradition.

All this is lodged in my head side-by-side with Ronsard's sonnets, the poems of Toulet or Apollinaire, the sonnets of Shakespeare, Racine's tirades, Montaigne's reflections, the verse of Kalidasa, or the aphorisms of the samkhya philosophy.

This medley forms the "database" on which my thought is formulated: it also fashions my mind when I am not using it directly. Some of these texts have, in my case, been in written form, but they had been prepared orally before being transcribed. Writing is only a means of fixing, useful but transitory, which is not indispensable. It is merely a way of storing an episode of my thought, just as the vegetables from my kitchen garden, kept in the refrigerator, are the fruit of agriculture and are only transmitted through this cold storage.

In societies that follow the oral tradition, poets and thinkers transmit their creation directly to the memory of their chosen audience. A recent example of this is the great Indian poet Rabindranath Tagore. At night, he invented his poems and the tune that would accompany them.

In the morning, he taught them to his disciples, who immediately memorized them. Their later transcription, the words of which were exact, never quite matched the diction and the melodic subtlety, which meant that degeneration set in rapidly. The result has been a clash between those who maintain that the highly inferior written version is the real one, and those who perpetuate the oral tradition.

WRITING STERILIZES INSPIRATION

Attempts to reduce to written form the traditional knowledge of countries that have always belonged to the oral tradition paralyze its continuity, its development, and only provide a partial view. The ethnologist transcribes a few odds and ends of knowledge from a bard, takes it over, and steals his role and livelihood, rather as if you were to burn the rest of the books after choosing one in a library, on the grounds that you have extracted the essential.

The parallel with music is interesting. In societies belonging to the oral tradition, so long as music is improvised—meaning that the discourse develops, like the art of oratory, according to a given theme corresponding to an idea, a feeling, an image, utilizing for the purpose a chosen vocabulary that is modal and rhythmic, within a metric framework—the musician develops his theme with eloquence, fantasy, humor, and passion. If you attempt to write it down and play it on the basis of the written music, disaster strikes. If it even approaches exactitude, the written version is extremely complicated, practically unreadable, leading inevitably to a melodic and rhythmic simplification that damages the modal meaning and makes it impossible to develop the theme.

Traditional music is endangered and dies as soon as it is transcribed and performed on the basis of its transcription. It is the same with literature, epic poems, myths, and legends, of which writing claims to establish a form that itself varies by nature. The mental structures of living memory are the antithesis of the mechanical nature of the written word. The Western musician has, in less than two centuries, lost the aptitude to continue *ad libitum* a structure initiated in music, thus eliminating a way of thinking that goes from inside to outside, as in Indian music.

Things are not very different in the case of literary or poetic thought. Poetry, the tool for transmitting knowledge, tends nowadays, in the West, to become a word play of no great importance. You need a great actor to breathe life into a text learned and long studied and repeated. This has nothing to do with the inflammatory oratory of the popular speaker, which develops and casts a spell for hours over its listeners, which when transcribed may appear mediocre, boring, inconsistent. We have this sort of experience on reading interview transcripts.

READING

Reading, the decoding of the written message, is a technique that concerns those for whom the message was written. A book of higher mathematics is, for me, totally incomprehensible. In such a case, I am illiterate. At the same time, I can't stop an involuntary irritation when a secretary makes a mistake in transcribing a Sanskrit word: "That fool doesn't know what he's writing!" The fact is that one is only literate in a particular system and within certain limits.

Highly developed intelligence apart—a specialization that often goes hand in hand with disabilities of a practical kind—the fact of reading does not improve our thought circuits, but encumbers them with data of no value, to the detriment of the individual's balance and of his real, usable store of knowledge.

SCRIBES

Until recently, even in Europe, most people were unable to write. For this purpose, there were scribes, public writers, a not very highly considered caste. Many great kings, famous strategists, religious reformers, and patrons of the arts, who forged our society, were illiterate, including the early emperors of China, as well as Charlemagne and Ashoka.

At the beginning of the seventeenth century, India's great Mogul Emperor, Akbar, impassioned about religion and philosophy, summoned the scholars and thinkers of every sect, presided over their debates, and himself created a new syncretic religion. He knew neither how to read nor write. Writing was a profession for artisans, unsuited to the well born.

Scribes have long formed an artisan caste whose profession is writing, just as that of the laundrymen is to wash clothes, or that of the potter to manufacture urns. The scribe is not a holder of knowledge. He is an artisan, used by knowledge or power, just as the mason who builds a temple is not its architect.

THE DICTATORSHIP OF THE SCRIBES

The identification of culture with reading and writing is a very recent phenomenon, one that has been a factor in the destruction of civilizations that have preserved, through oral tradition, a heritage of human knowledge and experience many thousands of years old. Thus the dictatorship of the scribes came about, officials who became the tools of state power.

Having become a schoolmaster, the scribe utilizes a sclerotic language as an instrument of tyranny and of the affirmation of his power, paralyzing its development, in parallel with that of science and morals. Nowadays, with their scorn and ignorance, the scribes crush the unhappy illiterate, who may be a carpenter or cabinet maker or mason, knowing all the secrets of those difficult professions. The country-woman knows how to utilize hundreds of plants for medicine or food. The wise woman's remedies are scornfully rejected until the writing fiends discover some that will profit the pharmaceutical industry, since the illiterate can claim no patent rights. The countryman knows the secrets of the seasons, the art of cuttings, the needs of plants, but is treated as an imbecile when he is forced to do his military service.

There is no need to insist on the cultural disaster resulting from the colonization of peoples belonging to the oral tradition by the attitude of superiority of ignorant and stupid conquerors who know how to read and write. In the modern world, the spread of words or formulas, the meaning or content of which are understood by very few, has led to verbal superstition, a kind of sanctification of certain words, which has become an amazing tool for manipulating human masses. This is the case of the "religions of the book"—certain phrases from the Vedas, the Bible, the Koran, or Marx are taken as "Gospel truth"—as well as modern catchwords such as Democracy, Fascism, Apartheid, Racism, Socialism, Liberalism, and Communism, fetishes serving to stir up the crowds who know neither their meaning nor their implications.

ELIMINATION OF ILLITERACY

Campaigns to eliminate illiteracy, which are fortunately not very effective, allow mediocre scribes to humiliate and demoralize entire peoples, to devalue their culture and knowledge, creating an anonymous proletariat where before there was a whole body of knowledge, myths, beliefs, social conventions, and a philosophy of life shared among the representatives of society's various essential functions.

This is why we see African ex-corporals—having learned to read and write in the French Army—becoming heads of state and using their superiority to crush the soothsayers, sorcerers, bards, the bearers of ancient and precious knowledge, the value of which will only be recognized when a scribe has transcribed some of its data.

For a considerable part of my life, I lived in a world characterized, on one side, by great men of letters and wise philosophers, and on the other, by the population as a whole, knowing neither how to read nor write and utilizing for their correspondence the services of a public letter-writer, which did not hinder them from living their cultural, religious, and ethical traditions with vivacity and intelligence.

I have never had feelings of intellectual superiority in my dealings with the little world of artisans, boatmen, musicians, peasants. On the contrary, I have often admired their lively spirit, their curiosity about ways of thinking, social ideals, and religious beliefs, their common sense, their knowledge in the most widely differing sectors, and the traditional virtues to which they were attached.

In a house in the Himalayas where I spent the summer, I took with me my servants from Benares. I noted that they held interminable discussions with the local shepherds, who were very skilful in playing the flute, meaning that they possessed all the elements of a refined art. I discreetly listened to one of their palavers. That day, the subject was the *Ramayana* legend, which they all knew without ever having seen it in writing. In it, Sita—the wife of the hero Rama, the incarnation of Vishnu—was kidnapped by the demon Ravana. They were discussing questions such as "How could the god allow Ravana to act like this? Is there therefore a limit to divine power? Or is the existence of evil a necessary counterpart to the existence of good?" Many theologians have found such problems difficult to answer.

I considered the difference between this illiterate talk and what I heard at the homes of my "educated" neighbors, who spoke of nothing but politics, current events, and articles from the papers. Where did the real culture lie?

I met with this difference again in the Italian village where I now live. My cook—who just about knows how to make out the headlines of the local paper and has never read an article—is renowned for his culinary art. He is also a skillful and wily negotiator, an indefatigable storyteller, full of humor, a person who counts in local politics. He judges the intrigues of the local politicians—who occasionally buy his vote—with serenity and common sense. Like many Italian "men of the people," he has a sense of honor, of hospitality, friendship, and justice, even if he is officially an illiterate and thus the designated victim of lawyers, judges, officials, and all the scribes puffed up with their superiority.

The general ability to read and write is above all a tool of propaganda and advertising which is now being displaced by television images and talks. It is merely a means of transmitting knowledge in specialist sectors, among people with the same interests, the same profession, utilizing the same language. It is at the same time a terrible means of establishing the scribes' domination and tyranny. It is their dictatorship that has created the illiterate.

Knowing how to read and write, a powerful tool of political

propaganda, is in many cases only a very relative benefit. At all events, it is a means of cultural destruction that can be highly effective. I cannot even be sure that the spread of reading and writing beyond a limited group of true scholars has served any other purpose than to assure the dictatorship of the scribes.

But those who have attained that position are not necessarily exceptionally gifted. Quite the opposite! The social illusion—which deceives the worker, panel beater, or fitter into thinking that it is he who builds the car, whereas he is merely a tool, a living interchangeable robot, used by the engineer who conceives the whole design—attains its highest point with the scribe who becomes an official, the interchangeable tool of the state who, like the busybody, gives himself a ridiculous and often pernicious importance. He persecutes us all with forms to be filled in, tax returns, mandatory accounts that take up precious time which could be better employed in other ways (everyone is illiterate when confronted with the gibberish of their forms).

This is one of the most odious phenomena of our time and probably one of the most destructive elements of our universal heritage of thought, technology, and the dignity of traditional knowledge. You can see the treatment meted out to an illiterate gypsy who possesses a prodigious violin technique, the centuries-old tradition of a highly refined art.

Language is the living basis of culture. It becomes enfeebled and loses its vigor and flavor if it becomes a stereotype. French is a language that has suffered particularly from writing, which tends to destroy the richness and creativity of local dialects and languages. This is clear in colonized countries where the imposition of French has destroyed not only the local languages, but also the philosophic, social, ethical, and theological concepts tied to a particular terminology. Instead of enriching itself with new concepts, French has wiped out the cultural heritage of the countries where it is imposed, including its own metropolitan territory. Similar attempts at fixing a literary and scholarly language have probably occurred in other cultures. The fixing of the French language is a recent example of providing a certain uniformity, but one that tends to paralyze linguistic development.

The case of the United States is different. Its people, comprising linguistically heteroclite elements, has long avoided the imposition of linguistic academism, which is why it is the only Western country where language remains alive and creates the words needed by modern developments. It is a spoken language that is only written down later on, with a terminology we are all obliged to borrow in the end. A large part of the people of the United States, although they may know how to read and write, are—from the point of view of their common language, English—illiterate. At home, a great number of Americans speak orally transmitted dialects, whether Yiddish, Irish, Sardinian, Sicilian, Chinese, Japanese, Dutch, Spanish, Portuguese, or Creole French.

A vast sector of the common tongue—English—since it is the language of no one in particular, is uncontaminated by any kind of academism and the burden of the written word, which has made it the most creative language in the modern world. New words are not invented by clerks; they are the discoveries of workers, mechanics, gold prospectors, miners, and farmers, over whom academic purists have no hold. The new words proposed by the scribes are as a rule stupid, artificial, and ineffective. Writing's predominance tends to sterilize language, whose development in certain countries has been paralyzed as a result of the importance attributed to writing. The consequences of this phenomenon have not been properly assessed.[1]

The Castes in Modern India

A t the outset of its regained independence, India was governed by politicians who had, in order to fight the invader on his own ground, made enormous efforts to soak up Western methods and forms of thought. They were probably the people best suited to save their country's independence in the midst of international conflict. Their whole training, however, set them against India's traditional institutions, which they did their best to destroy. Their efforts led only to disorder. It is possible to impose social legislation that is contrary to the laws of Manu, but people cannot be forced to observe it. From the state's point of view, caste distinctions can be suppressed in order to create a democratic society of the Western type, but this will not maintain the balance between the privileges and duties of each corporation. No caste can be forced to abandon its traditions, its customs, forms of initiation, and its own marriage and inheritance systems.

In a decentralized society like that of the Hindus, there is no practical hold over the thinking of the masses unless it goes in the same direction. Employing force is not a practical option, since the people involved form ninety-five percent of a population that knows what it thinks, unlike that of other countries. In any case, nothing can be done about the initiatic transmission of the Sannyasis, who are still the country's spiritual and moral guides, whose network covers the whole peninsula, from Nepal to Cape Comorin.

Notwithstanding invasions and efforts to impose foreign concepts on India, the Hindu hierarchy has been in no way affected, since in village cottages and in forest huts, as well as in cities and palaces, initiation is transmitted from father to son, from master to disciple. In the form of concise aphorisms learned by heart, the rites and texts can defy the centuries without leaving any physical trace. It was only certain externals of Hindu tradition that appeared to have been effaced during the foreign occupation—first Muslim, then European—which, in northern India, lasted nearly a thousand years. Tradition, and the form of society that maintains it, were not really affected.

The problems faced nowadays by India's governors are immense. Other countries may help India to recover. They may also, out of appreciation for and interest in Hindu culture and institutions, facilitate measures to safeguard the framework of a tradition that has been attacked with the greatest violence in the name of what the West calls progress. Hindu tradition cannot be lost, but it can only open its treasures to other peoples insofar as they help maintain it.

The West and the Merchant Caste

No society exists in which the four castes are not represented in one form or another. If their privileges and advantages are not properly balanced, and do not correspond to their aptitudes, and if they do not receive appropriate ethical training, the result is social disorder. If a society refuses to recognize the existence of different human types, to respect, manage, and control them, it can only explode. The castes will form again in any case, but on irrational bases, producing an unstable and erratic society. New intellectuals launch out on negative and absurd philosophies. War heroes, whose soldierly virtues of bravery are not employed, become the chiefs of red or black brigades, ready to sacrifice their own life and that of others in the name of a vague ideal, totally unrealizable and irrational. On their side, the merchants become rapacious and dishonest, seeking to seize political power with a view to gain. The artisans, exploited and envious, detest their work.

This is what Manu explains in his treatise on politics, written nearly three thousand years ago. He adds that when the rights of the castes are not recognized and balanced, the inevitable result is four sorts of tyranny in succession: the tyranny of priests or the churches, followed by military dictatorship, after which the tradesmen seize power, and then finally the dictatorship of the working classes.

We live in a society currently dominated by merchants. We consequently attempt to see all problems from an economic point of view. We shall then give power to incompetent worker representatives, and then to imbecilic colonels. Despite every effort made to create an anonymous and more easily exploited proletariat, most people in India are still attached to their caste, to their social and racial group, just as elsewhere people remain attached to their religious or linguistic group. However, it is more difficult for such groups to coexist nowadays, owing to the lack of any legislation that recognizes and protects their rights and privileges. The castes need each other, and no society can function if they do not share the work and respect each other.

In Western countries, castes inevitably exist because they are essential organs of the social body, but since they have no recognized and delimited identity and rights, they must always be on the defensive. We live in a world of every man for himself, in which the isolated individual has to defend himself and is envious of others' advantages. Duties and privileges are not coordinated, minorities are not protected and easily become the scapegoat for mistakes in state management. We continue to practice genocide on human groups who cannot or do not wish to adopt our way of life and our beliefs, as in the case of the American Indians, the Australians, the Pygmies, or—on occasion—the Jews and the gypsies.

We are in the worst position to criticize the caste institution, from which, on the other hand, we have much to learn.

Remarks on Cultural Colonization

Human beings are carnivores whose instinct is to protect and assure the hegemony of their species by destroying their adversaries. They exercise this instinct not only against other species, but also against other human groups.

Owing to the nature of the human animal itself, each tribe is always anxious to establish its supremacy. It only tolerates other groups if they have been subdued. The whole history of the human race, at every cultural level, is merely a series of conflicts to establish the domination of one more or less extended ethnic group over other groups, whether through the total destruction of its adversaries or—and here humans use their superior intelligence—by subjugating them so that they can be utilized to increase its greatness, its power, and its wealth.

Slavery was one of the main tools of material and intellectual greatness found in every ancient civilization, freeing the dominant group from the need for physical labor and providing it with the means and leisure to devote itself to activities other than those connected with its immediate survival.

Today, we know to what point brainwashing can destroy human personality. The forced adoption of a foreign culture, language, religion, or customs is merely a collective brainwashing, which equates to cultural genocide. At first, it may appear as a benefit, when the adopted culture seems more developed, more "advanced" than the recipient's native culture. It takes centuries, however, before such a character change has been sufficiently assimilated to allow peoples brutalized in their inner nature to contribute something original and valuable to culture as a whole. This is easily explained, since it appears that, in the long run, the aptitudes acquired by an ethnic group cause genetic changes in the collective character, leading to the blossoming of a given civilization. A culture change thus inevitably creates a state of inferiority whose outcome, at the level of imitation, will never be really creative.

This is very different from extending a person's culture by studying foreign languages and civilizations, once the child's early training has been completed in the context of its own native culture. Children who have acquired a perfect knowledge of their parents' language and then study a foreign language with a very different structure know how to use this language at quite another level than they would if they had studied it as their main language from their earliest years.

Whatever the benefits they believe they are bringing to the "underdeveloped" peoples they subjugate, colonial empires have no other aims than to obtain low-cost labor, a captive market, and territories they can exploit, while systematically destroying the way of life and culture of the colonized peoples. When certain peoples were not sufficiently profitable, genocide and expropriation were—and still are—practiced, as in the case of the American Indians, in certain areas of Africa, and the aboriginal peoples of Australia. Colonial settlements merely continued the practice of the major invasions of European proto-history.

The immensity of their empires and the impossibility for the "colonizers" wholly to replace the autochthonous peoples have, however, led to a more subtle policy. This consists of creating minority groups of "collaborators," detached from the mainstream population and entirely subjugated to foreign domination. The importing of the customs, language, and religion of the dominant power by limited groups of people in exchange for special privileges and semi-assimilation to the colonizing caste has led to the creation of wholly dependent persons who can be used as tools of domination. The Arabs and, later on, the Spaniards and Portuguese, coming to believe the religious coverage they had found for their political, economic, and commercial designs, made the mistake of insisting on mass conversions, giving the peoples a choice between death or adoption of the conquerors' religion and customs. By this very fact, they lost the tool of enduring power that consists of a minority at their service, slavishly sharing their contempt for the "pagans," their customs, beliefs, philosophy, and arts.

These artificial communities, speaking their language and familiar with their habits, quite naturally appeared to the Westerners as an easy form of contact between themselves and their former colonies (whether colonies in the political sense of the word, cultural colonies created by religious missions, or, more recently, by institutes of cultural propaganda). They constitute the remarkable source of false assessment of civilizations other than Western, whether in terms of social organization, economic reality, religion, art, philosophy, history, and so on. An example of this can be seen in the recent history of Vietnam. One of the elements in the Vietnamese war imbroglio was the protection of the privileges acquired by a Christianized minority, whose points of view were falsely considered to represent those of the people as a whole.

Such communities are often the ones to which the colonial powers transfer power and, in many cases, they have remained as the basis of actual governments in newly independent countries, since the maintaining of independence is tied to economic aid and consequently to easy contacts with Western powers. Thus—by means of the pressure exercised by its economic aid on peoples threatened by famine—the West keeps such governments in power. The consequences are catastrophic.

At an artistic level, all the countries of Asia and Africa, including the eastern Soviet Republics, are on the way to becoming sad suburbs of Europe and America, pitifully absorbing the out of date and mediocre forms of a foreign musical culture, at the same time as the West is beginning to discover the extraordinary value and artistic treasures of other civilizations.

Reversing the machinery of cultural propaganda is difficult, however, and cannot be done in a day. Some countries, like India, have already—to a great extent—realized that they have more to gain by preserving and exporting the values of their own culture than by seeking to play a role in Western culture.

This international rehabilitation of the cultural and artistic values of non-Western civilizations does not of course exclude a knowledge of Western art. This will, however, have to be matched by a widening of culture at the highest level and not, as is so often the case, by replacing a highly developed autochthonous culture with a foreign culture that can only be assimilated at its lowest level. The reasons for this are not solely a matter of education, which could to a certain extent be remedied, but the hereditary nature of the formulas on which the communication mechanisms of the human brain function.

Cultural Genocide in Africa

In order to define the position that the music of Africa can and should occupy in international music, we must first of all discard a certain number of concepts that tend to distort the approach of foreigners—and even of Africans themselves—to the history, nature, and values of African music.

Africa is not an isolated continent. It is not a far-distant island where prehistoric cultures have miraculously survived for musical archaeologists to study and classify, just as one studies and classifies various sorts of flints. The great cultural currents affecting other parts of the world have also been felt throughout the African continent, including: the more ancient ones connecting the Pygmies to the Munda cultures of India and of the Malayan-Indo-Chinese peninsula, which have also left traces in Europe; the ancient cultures of the Mediterranean world to which north Africa and a large part of Abyssinia belong, but which stretched much further; the culture of Islam, which had major centers as far as west Africa; and the Hindu culture of which Madagascar and east Africa were great centers, not to speak of more recent influences. Likewise, in all countries, at different epochs, we find the influence of African musical forms.

The problems of African music nowadays are no different from those of other continents. The enormous musical machine that developed at the same time as the industrial revolution in Europe, which passed—for a time—as the very expression of the material and cultural progress of humankind, culminating in the Wagnerian orchestra, has been the source of destruction for other forms of musical art that do not employ the piano and large orchestras as a means of expression. We have gradually had to rediscover Bach, Monteverdi, and Guillaume de Machaut, but the conception itself of the superiority of tempered polyphonic music, written down and orchestrated, continues to be the basis for a systematic destruction of all surviving forms of musical language in Europe, as on the other continents, together with an at times surprising lack of appreciation for artistic and linguistic musical values.

Projected onto Africa with the force of a colonialism as self-convinced as it was self-interested, such conceptions have quite naturally wholly disorientated the sense of values and disorganized the centers of musical life. Music—as it has developed over the past three or four centuries in Europe—is necessarily considered as representing the culmination of human genius, and this concept is imposed on the rest of the world with extraordinary arrogance. Whatever is not symphonic can only be a stammering folklore, arising as it were by spontaneous generation from the less developed strata of the human race: this is an old-fashioned romantic idea that can be justified by no fact at all.

Although colonialism has nowadays abandoned—in Africa as in other "third-world" countries—its most brutal forms of genocide and slavery, the concepts of cultural and racial superiority it used as its justification have not been sincerely revised. Appearances and methods have changed, but not the basic attitude. Cultural colonialism as a condition of economic aid has become a more subtle weapon of domination. Importing a foreign culture among limited groups of people, in exchange for special privileges and a semi-assimilation to Western standards, has led to the creation of false elites formed entirely of persons depending on outside help, who are the perfect intermediaries for cultural domination. On musical and other levels, the consequences have been catastrophic. The initiatives taken or encouraged by the West are almost inevitably based on a false evaluation of realities, provided by those members of the population whose only chance of survival and of retaining their privileges depends on foreign support. It follows that despite the best intentions, most initiatives in cultural aid produce results that are the opposite of those intended.

The tiny Westernized minorities are still—owing to the facility of language relations and the habit of viewing matters on Western terms— the main contacts and applicants for the cultural programs of international organizations. Consequently, we should not be amazed if the efforts made by UNESCO, for example, tend to create miserable provincial orchestras or Western music schools of an abysmal level, rather than taking an interest in the great traditions of African musical art. Informants and counselors in the countries involved present "indigenous" musical culture as superseded folklore, interesting at the most to musical archaeologists seeking the vestiges of a long-vanished embryonic culture. The Western powers, major foundations, and international organizations are thus unaware that they are mightily contributing to the destruction of a large part of Africa's musical art in perfect good faith, since the Africans themselves, or at least those who speak in their name, advertise the benefits of the musical art of the West and its methods of teaching music.

Efforts made over the past decades by Western specialists and their African pupils to study African music have often been based on serious conceptual errors, in particular the confusion of racial and cultural matters. The idea that a form of sound expression is tied to a particular species may be valid for different sorts of bird, but it is not so for human beings. There is no doubt that race affects certain characteristics of our sensitivity, that a Finn will tend to create musical forms that are different from those of a Spaniard. But culture, by its very nature, does not heed these barriers and—although we can expect a certain color of artistic expression owing to racial characteristics—the bases of culture are never, on any continent, tied to race. The division of Africa into "ethnical groups" completely falsifies values from an overall cultural and artistic point of view. It is no more valid in Africa than it is in Europe. The very term "ethnomusicology," employed in the study of

African music, already implies taking a stand that is scientifically and culturally unacceptable.

What musical ethnology is seeking in Africa is, above all, the "primitive." We should know to what extent the notion of "primitive" can be misleading. The appearance of human beings on earth did not occur yesterday. Even among peoples who nowadays live in extremely simple conditions, we find no spoken language that is not the outcome of an extremely long evolution and complex development, allowing the most abstract ideas to be expressed. It is difficult to see how it could be otherwise in the case of musical language. What is studied as being "primitive" is, as often as not, a vestige, a simplified and degenerate survival that has nothing to do with any so-called archaic art. This is totally clear even in the structural bases of popular musical idioms.

What is recorded as primitive folklore is usually merely the form—reduced to bare essentials—of out-of-date songs that have lost their own musical context. One French radio program each morning phones postal workers, shorthand typists, and provincial butchers and asks them to sing a song. The result is, as a rule, a song by Gilbert Bécaud or Sylvie Vartan, caterwauled in a mediocre fashion, which in effect corresponds—in its relation to the original—to what ethnologists and folklore enthusiasts too often piously collect from villagers as compared to the music's ancient origins. Furthermore, folklore is taken to include whatever differs from classical Western idiom, even when it is at a very high professional and artistic level. The total lack of any understanding of values leads to the absurd treatment meted out to the great musical traditions still surviving in Africa, which are arranged to fabricate false folklore, folklore for tourists, and other aberrations that are just as rife elsewhere. Claims are made of noting forms with an unknown system of reference; vague melodic outlines are subsequently taught in a pretentious fashion, as aberrant as they are mediocre, while claiming to "save national folklore."

Instead of orienting research toward what may be termed a "research into lack of culture," an effort should be made, with the collaboration of the cultural organizations of African countries, to make a

systematic assessment of the major cultural currents that have contributed to the development of the musical forms encountered on the
continent, a serious study of the forms of musical language and musical communication still existing there, as well as of any original artistic
performances that are their expression. For this purpose, an overall
study of the African continent will have to be made, disregarding state
borders, ethnic and linguistic groups, in order to seek—after the cultural crisis caused by the colonial period—the highest artistic and technical survivals of musical forms that are peculiar to Africa, and to give
them the place they deserve in the musical creation of our time.

We are gradually witnessing the disappearance, before the influx of
musical concepts imported from the West, of musical language forms
with a universal value, but which, in their own country, are considered
and treated as "folklore" survivals, at the most good for being
"arranged" according to today's tastes. This will lead to the destruction
of their whole value as works of art and as original means of communication, and thus of their universal interest.

Relations Between the Dravidian and African Negro Cultures

This paper is a working hypothesis. It is an extension to sub-Saharan Africa of the research I am carrying out on the influence of the pre-Aryan Dravidian civilization on the civilizations of the Middle East and the Mediterranean countries, at anthropological, linguistic, religious, ritual, mythological, and social levels. An overall approach is, in fact, essential to obtain convincing results.

It is clear that a very great civilization—with the Dravidian language and the Shaivite religion as its vehicle—forms an essential component of all later civilizations in India and the Mediterranean countries. My research has led me to recognize the fact that this influence extended as far as pre-Celtic northern Europe. Similarly, it appears that a considerable part of the African continent must have belonged to the same vast culture. However, in regions where stone is not the main building material, archaeological evidence is practically nonexistent and history is obliterated, as in the case both of Africa and Indochina. We know that highly refined civilizations existed for thousands of years, yet history reduces them to a few centuries. Investigation is thus limited to matching archaeological, ethnic, and linguistic evidence. As far as Africa is concerned, studies have so far been very fragmentary and discontinuous. African studies should all start from the assumption of African participation in this great protohistoric Dravidian civilization. I am convinced the results would be astonishing.

In the African world, we also have to face an additional problem: Islamic and subsequently Christian absolutism and the puritanism that is peculiar to these Semitic religions have thrown such discredit on the institutions, beliefs, rites, and gods of earlier religions—whatever their philosophic or human values—that there is a widespread tendency to ignore, reject, or dissimulate any survivals of ancient customs and beliefs. This obstacle has to be overcome if we wish to uncover the ties that may have united the Dravidian world with Africa, since such ties are clearly much earlier than modern religions. It is most important for prejudice to be left aside, if we wish to discover the common sources of the African civilizations and ancient Dravidian culture.

HISTORICAL FACTS

The Aryan cultural invasion—which began during the third millennium before the current Western era and has continued down to our own times—is an extraordinary phenomenon in the history of humankind. Relatively primitive tribes from central Asia managed to impose their language on a large part of the human race. This invasion of languages of Aryan origin, which supplanted all the original languages of northern India, Russia, Persia, and the whole of Europe, has in modern times extended to the American continent and subsequently to Africa, where English, French, Spanish, and Portuguese have become the predominant languages.

A similar phenomenon, though less extensive, was the Arab conquest, which assimilated the numerous ethnic groups of the Middle East and the African continent, its religious influence extending much further than its linguistic conquest. The case of Buddhism was similar. In India, its vehicular language—Pali—had only a limited influence, whereas its concepts have influenced the entire Far East.

Everywhere, conquerors assimilate a considerable part of the culture of the lands they have conquered. A very large portion of Hindu civilization comes from pre-Aryan cultures, from those splendid cities ferociously destroyed by the Aryan nomads, spoken of with such contempt by their most ancient texts, rather like those armed tribes reigning today over Cambodia, when they speak of the vanished population of Phnom Penh.

We know that the conquering Achaeans learned professions and arts from the women of the decimated Pelasgians or Cretans, and that what we call the Greek civilization largely comes from the peoples conquered by the Achaean, then Dorian, Aryans. The same happened in the Arab world and many elements of Islamic civilization come from previous cultures—Egyptian, Roman, Greek, Persian, Phoenician, Syrian, and so on. What we know as Arab music is a typical case. It is music of Greco-Persian origin, and is totally different from the original musical tradition of Arabia as such.

Proud of their power, the conquerors rarely acknowledged their debt to the conquered peoples and sought to deny or dissimulate their sources. This is why it is so difficult to reestablish historical reality. One of the most refined and durable civilizations—that of Egypt on the African continent—is often treated by historians as a relatively isolated and marginal phenomenon, as compared to European or African cultures.

The documents we possess on ancient Dravidian culture, besides highly important linguistic and religious survivals and archaeological data, are very numerous, including, in particular, the Shaivite *Puranas* in Tamil, or in their Sanskrit versions. These historical-mythical texts, rather like the Bible—although they have been recast much later—contain precious material on ancient Shaivism and the history of humankind. The same goes for the somewhat esoteric *Agamas* and *Tantras*, which have more or less secretly preserved the rites and beliefs of ancient Shaivism, notwithstanding Aryan domination.

LANGUAGES

Any language is the outcome of a very long evolution at a conceptual level, bearing witness to extremely developed philosophic and ritual notions. Influences are felt more especially at the level of vocabulary, whereas certain structural elements prove to be very durable, since they are related to thought mechanisms.

Agglutinative languages, known as Dravidian, are now spoken in southern India, but it appears that a Dravidian language was the cultural tongue of the whole of northern India, where Aryanized languages are spoken today. The latter have, however, preserved—as remarked by Suniti Kumar Chatterji—Dravidian infrastructures, as in the case of Hindi, Marathi, Bengali, Pahar, and others. It is almost certain that the language spoken in the ancient cities of the Indus valley, destroyed by the Vedic Aryan invaders, belonged to the Dravidian family. An enclave of Dravidian language still exists in Beluchistan. These languages, which are not necessarily of Indian origin, were apparently—at a certain period—the cultural languages of a large part of the world, stretching from India to the Mediterranean and the Atlantic. Survivals of Dravidian languages are found all around the Mediterranean world. The most important are Caucasian Georgian, Peuhl (as shown by recent research), and, in all probability, Basque. Ancient authors considered that Pelasgian, Lydian, Etruscan, and Carthaginian belonged to the same family. Turkish and Finno-Ugrian are a distant branch of the same linguistic group. The aim of this study is to discover how far Dravidian languages and culture penetrated the African continent.

Contacts with Dravidian India and East Africa on the one hand, and with the Dravidian Mediterranean and North Africa on the other, stem from the remotest times. A study of the various languages and dialects of the African continent and any linguistic relationships with the Dravidian world has still to be carried out. It cannot be excluded that Dravidian substrates may be found in languages belonging to other families, as in the case of those spoken in northern India. Research must consequently assume a Dravidian basis. Lastly, it has been suggested that some of the peoples of southern India—who according to their own tradition came from a lost continent to the south-west of Cape Comorin—might be of African origin.

TRADE

Since time immemorial, the east coast of Africa, the Socotra Isles, Bahrain, and southern Arabia have been the centers for trade coming from India, Indonesia, and the Far East, the goods being subsequently transshipped and sent toward Phoenicia, Egypt, Crete, and—later on—the Roman world, as well as to Ethiopia and the various African empires. The means of transport must have been highly developed even from an extremely early period, since teak from the Malabar coast was employed in building some of the Babylonian temples. Ancient navigators were familiar with the monsoons, which the Arabs and Europeans discovered only later on. In ancient times, every week several ships would arrive from the ports of southern India, carrying cloth, spices, pottery, and precious stones to the prosperous cities of east Africa, of which only a few ruins still exist. The pharaohs had dug a canal from Klysma near Suez to facilitate cargoes bound for the Mediterranean.

Later on, the Romans enacted a law limiting imports from the East and from Africa, which were draining Roman gold reserves. A Greek play discovered on an Egyptian papyrus deals with a shipwreck on the Indian coast, with some of the characters speaking Kanada, one of the main Dravidian languages of the west coast of India. This clearly implies that the language was fairly well known and was not regarded as some kind of incomprehensible jargon.

The main ports of the Zandj coast of east Africa in historical times, such as Lamou, Paté, Malindi, Mombassa, Zanzibar, and Kiloa, carried on considerable trade with southern India, importing cloth and pottery and exporting to Arabia and India ivory, wax, slaves, and, above all, gold from the mines of Zimbabwe. We know little about the rich African empires of former times, and many names of cities mentioned by the Hebrews, Egyptians, Greeks, and Indians still have to be identified.

ANTHROPOLOGY

From an anthropological point of view, the Pygmies and Bushmen are related to the Paleolithic peoples of the Caucasus and the Munda tribes in India. At the same time, skeletons of the Gangetic type are found in predynastic tombs in Egypt, also related to certain races in western Africa or Ethiopia. It has been suggested that the Hamitic peoples share a common origin with many Europeans. There is nothing to show that white human beings are European, or that black ones have African origins. We have recently witnessed the almost total substitution of populations both on the American continent and in Australia, with the result that populations—whether major groups or small minorities—can only be studied on a worldwide scale.

RELIGION

The most lasting influences are felt at the level of religion, customs, and rites. In northern India, religion derives—in theory—from Aryan Vedism. In actual fact, however, most of the beliefs, rites, and philosophic or cosmological concepts, myths, and so on are of Dravidian origin.

In pre-Aryan India, we find a god of nature and of the forest called Mayan or Annal. Later on, he was known as Pashupati (Lord of the Animals) or Shiva (the Benevolent), connected with the phallus, bull, and snake cults. We find images of this ithyphallic horned god, surrounded by animals, on the seals discovered at Mohenjo Daro (about 2000 B.C.E.). Among the Ashantis of Africa, the same forest deities are found, as well as a horned god similar to the one encountered in the Indus civilization.

Shiva is surrounded by Ganas, joker-spirits who play tricks on both gods and men. The African Anansi is also a playful god. His sexual organ is detachable, like Shiva's, and the result is a thousand adventures. It is difficult not to compare the sacred images of Lagba Yoruba with the erect organ of ithyphallic Shiva and his emblem, the *linga* (phallus).

The most ancient Dravidian deity is a young god called Murugan (the boy), or Velan (he of the boar-spear), or Seyyan (the red), dwelling among the mountains and associated with the cult of the cock and the peacock. He may originally have been independent of the Lord of the Animals but, in mythological accounts, Murugan is Shiva's son and their rites are extremely entwined, in the form of a cult found throughout the Mediterranean world. Shiva-Pashupati corresponds to Cretan Zan, later called Zagreus, who was then mistaken for the Aryan Zeus. Murugan is called Dionysos (the God of Nysa), from the name of the mountain on which he dwells. Greek authors often locate this mountain on the African continent. In Egypt, Dionysos is called Osiris.

Phallic Cults

A characteristic feature of Shaivite philosophy must here be mentioned: sensual enjoyment, pleasure that is the image of divine beatitude. Fecundity is only a by-product. Sexual union is thus seen as participating in the divine state and, in this sense, the images that represent it have a sacred value and play a protective role. The antisexual prejudices of Semitic religions have led to the disregarding of its profound symbolism and to puerile and vulgar interpretations, seeing it at all costs—and in an entirely arbitrary manner—as "fertility rites."

Phallic monuments identical to those in India (the erect phallus, sometimes with a face, surrounded by a serpent) are found throughout the Western world, in Mediterranean countries, and as far as pre-Celtic England, as also in Africa. Phallic emblems mounted on an *arghya* (female organ), practically identical to those of India, are found both in Zaire and Nigeria. Sculpted phallic shaped monoliths—even three or four meters high and decorated with engraved symbols—are found in the Sudama and Borama valleys, in the south of Ethiopia, and on the islands close to Somalia, as well as in Tanganyika. These monuments are always connected with the Shiva-Dionysos cults that are undoubtedly of Dravidian origin. Shaivites wear a small *lingam* (phallus) around their neck, a practice found also in Zimbabwe.

Dances

Cult features include ecstatic dances, festivals in which the deities are portrayed by masked persons (whence their survival in Western carnivals), and orgiastic rites in which taboos are lifted. Great license is permitted and sexual rites are practiced. Similar examples of ceremonial freedom, so widely practiced in the Dionysian world, are also found in Africa.

Collective forms of ecstatic and prophetic dance met with in southern India are wholly identical both in form and technique to the Greek dithyramb and to the *zikr* of Islamic brotherhoods. These dances, which induce a state of trance, are very widespread in the Dravidian world, providing a way of contacting the spirits and prophesizing. Descriptions of this can be found in the *Shilappadikaram*, the Tamil novel of the third century C.E. The dances played an important role in the Dionysian *Mania*, as well as being found among the Ashantis, in Dahomey, and even in the Antilles. Such dances are still practiced nowadays.

Nudity

The god Shiva is shown naked, his body smeared with ash or with plaster. His followers do the same. These naked ascetics, their bodies covered with ash, can still be encountered in India today. As Marcel Detienne remarks, "The Titans who seized Zeus are beings covered with plaster. . . . This troupe of masked men covered with plaster surround the young boy, recalling in a surprising manner the adults in African societies, transformed into supernatural beings by a layer of whitish earth."[1] Ritual nakedness appears as an essential trait in many ancient cults.

Animal Deities

The bull is Shiva's sacred animal, his vehicle. The bull is Shiva. Dionysos is also a bull god who appears in bull form.

The cock, together with the peacock, is the sacred animal of Murugan, a god who requires sacrifices. The cock sacrifice, so widespread in Africa and among the African peoples of the Caribbean, recalls the same cult.

It has been noted that many traits of Egyptian religion are related to those of black Africa, such as: the cults of half-man, half-animal beings; deified kings; cults of manly strength; as well as of the after-life, including offerings for the dead, and so on. But these features are the very ones that are characteristic of Shaivism. We have only to think of Nandi, the bull represented with a man's body, or Ganapati, with his elephant's head. The images of the Cretan Minotaur are identical to those of Nandi.

In ritual dances, masks evoke those divine beings that put humans back in their place among the other creatures in a world where plants, animals, humankind, genies, and gods find their fundamental unity and interdependence in the wonderful harmony of Creation.

As Lord of the Animals, Shiva is represented as a horned god. Horns are a symbol of domination, of royalty, of ancestral greatness. This concept may be compared with the horned masks with which the Dogons evoke their ancestors. Masks have magic power. In the Kathakali theater of southern India, the actor—once masked—becomes the deity he represents. He may no longer be treated as a human being, nor called by any other name than that of the god. The same occurs in Africa.

Initiation

Initiation rites play an essential role in Shaivism. They are described in detail in the *Shiva Purana* and the *Linga Purana*. Initiation constitutes a death, after which the initiate is reborn as an adult capable of varying responsibilities. The same definition can be given to the initiation rites of the Ba Pende in southern Zaire.

Initiation rites are secret and thus lead to the formation of secret societies. Such societies are religious groups allowing contacts with the spirit world, but also create social hierarchies. Secret societies of this kind are found among the Shaivite associations practicing Tantric rites and Indian Bhakta groups, as well as among the Dionysian Bacchant associations and related sects down to our own times. Parallels are evident with the great African secret societies like the Poros in western Africa. Like the Shaivite associations, African societies go beyond the limits of caste or tribe.

Sacrifices

The Creator has fashioned a cruel world where nothing can survive without devouring other lives. "I am he who devours and is devoured," says the god of the *Taittiriya Upanishad*. The gods thirst for blood and, to satisfy their thirst, victims must be offered to them in order to limit their destructive power, ritualizing and consecrating the act by which one living being inexorably devours another.

The sacrifices of bulls, buffaloes, and goats in our own times still play an essential role in popular Shaivism, just as they did in the Dionysian cult. The Aissaoua sects in Morocco practice sacrifices accompanied by homophagy (the eating of raw sacrificial meat) and ecstatic dances, directly inherited from Dionysian practices. The concept of sacrifice, when used to ritualize martial deeds—the struggle between human groups (which is also part of natural law)—can even involve anthropophagy. Human sacrifices are mentioned in Shaivite texts, and are also encountered in the Cretan and Greek Dionysian world, whether as the victims offered to the Minotaur, the sacrifice of Iphigenia, or of Pentheus torn to pieces by the Maenads in Euripides' *Bacchantes*. Much has to be reconsidered in rites of this kind met with in African civilizations, the symbolism of which has been very badly presented. To my knowledge, Euripides is not deemed to be a barbarian, yet Agave, in her ritual exaltation, devours the raw flesh of her own son. We should not forget that the Christian ritual—a survival of the Dionysian rite—symbolically evokes the consumption of the divine victim.

Rites

Funerary rites must also be studied, since in the Dravidian-Shaivite world, the dead are placed in underground chambers with the accessories they will need in the next world. The dead person is conveyed to his dwelling with dancing and manifestations of joy. The Aryans, on the other hand, burned their dead and lamented. The parallel between the Egyptians and Dravidians is clear, and it is to this group that Africa's numerous funerary rites belong.

The deities of India can be represented by magic diagrams, or *yantras*, which are used as cult objects. They can easily be compared with the complex diagrams utilized in rituals in Dahomey and Haiti.

Perhaps we should also mention the rites by means of which subtle powers can be launched against enemies. Such rites, known as Aghora in the Shaivite tradition, are found in western Africa, and are called Obeah in Haiti and Jamaica.

CONCLUSION

Comparative studies of the languages, customs, religions, rites, mythology, and philosophy of the various peoples of black Africa, and their relations with the Dravidian world, would clearly give highly important results, given the importance of the Egyptian civilization and its influence well beyond the Sudan (the Tuaregs still use a writing system derived from Egyptian), the relations over thousands of years between Dravidian India and eastern Africa, the immense spread of cults related to Dravidian Shaivism and to Murugan, the strong influence of Indianized Indonesia and India on Madagascar and southern Africa, the penetration of Shaivism—in its Dionysian form—to the south of the Sahara, and the fact that Carthaginian and Peuhl are known to be languages of Dravidian origin.

Although the little research carried out on relations between Europe and Mediterranean and Middle Eastern countries has everywhere revealed Dravidian origins or influence, it is not at all certain that the Dravidian civilization and its religious conceptions are of Indian origin. According to their own tradition, the peoples of southern India came from the sea. The most ancient peoples of India speak Munda languages. We can merely state that, starting from the seventh millennium before our era, a vast civilization speaking Dravidian languages stretched from India to the Atlantic. The fact that, in India, only the southern regions have been able to resist Aryanization, despite constant efforts still carried out even today (such as the imposition of Sanskrit, Pali, Persian, English, Hindi), is largely due to its privileged geographical location. This does not at all imply, however, that India was the first base of the Dravidian peoples, or of the Shaivite religion.

Certain anthropological elements indicate African relationships. In Europe, Christianity did everything possible to wipe out its sources, even though—like Brahmanism in India—it incorporated numerous Dionysian features, such as the god walking on the waters, changing water into wine, riding an ass, the choice (in the fourth century) of the timing of the feast of the Child Dionysos to celebrate the nativity of Christ, and so on. I am not competent to deal with African civilizations, but it does appear that major exchanges must have taken place.

A thorough study of the Dravidian civilization and the rites of the religion of Mayan–Annal–Nampan–Shiva–Zan–Zagreus on the one hand, and Murugan–Velan–Seyyan–Skanda–Dionysos on the other—not only in the attenuated and puritan practices of certain modern Shaivite sects, but in their often violent archaic forms—should serve as a point of departure for an understanding of African civilizations and religions and would bring fascinating results.

Rights and Duties

Since the seventeenth century, western Europe has seen the spread of a major movement directed by philosophers and humanists for greater human justice and a more equitable distribution of the necessities and joys of life. This movement led to the French Revolution and, little by little, to the Socialist revolutions, the independence of colonies, the emancipation of women, and the abolition of slavery.

It was always the thinkers, the sociologists and psychologists, who drew attention to the injustices rampant within what we know as the social order and suggested remedies that could be applied. A still-functioning nineteenth century organization, known as the League for Human Rights, often played an important role in indicating to legislators and public authorities what they deemed was the right of every man to a minimum of prosperity, justice, education, and so on.

These attainments are, however, far from being consolidated, coherent, and universally recognized. Furthermore, the extraordinary events that have upset the social and economic conditions of our time have changed the framework of life for almost everyone, forcing us to question the ideas and methods judged sufficient a mere century earlier to tackle social problems. A brutal, unstable society in constant transformation—such as our postindustrial society—poses new and serious problems that cannot be solved by means of past slogans.

Nowadays we are asked to make a choice of political systems, all of which have their defects, within nations claiming to assimilate or dominate all their foreign minorities, without ever managing to solve the question of what social justice is, or liberty, or the rights and duties of man as an individual, or the reciprocal tolerance of ethnic or religious groups with their distinct moral and social concepts. What should be the rights of a Jew or a Christian in an Arab country, or of a Muslim in a Christian country or in Israel? Is an individual more free or less badly treated in the United States according to his sympathies for bourgeois or communist ideology? Traces of the McCarthy persecution of communists and homosexuals are far from being erased. The Nazi suppression of any religious, racial, sexual, or political deviation, although pushed to the extreme, is also far from being an isolated phenomenon.

What meaning can freedom have without hope, or ambition without freedom, a right separated from duty, as in the case of so many young people in certain shantytowns? What do the rights of man matter without the means to fight against persecutions and genocides except by war or migration, which lead to the invasion and eventually the ruin of those countries that are more humanitarian than others?

No nation, no organized society, can host or assimilate persons who reject its laws, its conventions, and its notions of justice. A multiracial or multi-religious society cannot be founded on the famous "I ask from you in the name of your principles what I refuse to give you in the name of my own."

Any definition of the rights of man that is not balanced by duties takes no account of reality and can in no way be effective. It signifies covering with a veil of good intentions the injustices and persecutions of a society that claims to be free and egalitarian.

At the same time, do we ever make a real assessment of the rights of women or children, of adolescents or minorities, in each of our political systems? In some countries—not necessarily liberal regimes—woman is proclaimed to be man's equal, when she has neither the same strength nor social role, necessitating adjustments to take into account her functional peculiarities, her maternal role. She has a right to independence, to work, to divorce, to food aid, but such freedom often leads to the destruction of the family cell, and the mental distress of the children.

Elsewhere, women are prisoners, married against their will, stoned if found guilty of adultery. Elsewhere, they are victims of cruel sexual mutilations, elsewhere, sometimes even burned alive. In some countries, they are given a prison sentence if suspected of prostitution, or of encouraging it, according to the concepts to which the various religions give their sinister support.

The rights of the child and the adolescent are, as a rule, the least recognized, whether by democratic or totalitarian societies. In which country is an adolescent entitled to pursue his vocation and escape from the tyranny of hostile and uncomprehending parents? The extending of underage status up to eighteen years and obligatory schooling, sometimes in particularly repressive institutions, deprives him of any independence, after which he is delivered up to the tyranny of what is termed military service. In certain countries, this is out-and-out slavery, and can last for several years. The adolescent is only able to discover the world and exercise his talents when he becomes an adult, whereas adolescence is the period when his aspirations, his talents, and his spirit crystallize. In France today, a Mozart would never be able to achieve success as an infant prodigy, nor even produce most of his work. We all know of cases where talent has not been recognized, or has been victimized.

At a sexual level, adult jealousy of young males is a constant among most animal species. In those years in which the sexual impulse is at its peak—from 13 to 18 for man—repression is almost total, reducing erotic activity to sad masturbation, accompanied by fantasies from which some men never free themselves.

With regard to homosexuality as a component of adolescent sexuality, repression can reach such ferocious cruelty and incomprehension that it often fixes a tendency that may otherwise only be temporary. The persecution of homosexuality, which in some countries is punished by prison or death, deprives the adolescent of that adult affection and protection that is necessary for his harmonious development. In certain more liberal countries where intimate relations between persons of the same sex has recently been allowed between adults, it is as a rule forbidden between an adult and a minor, whatever the latter's sexual maturity.

Regions or states containing peoples who are different because of their beliefs or origins—such as autochthonous minorities like Protestants and Catholics in Ireland, Kurds and other ethnic groups in Iraq, or Jews and Palestinians in Israel—face problems of freedom and rights that are not properly defined.

We proclaim the right of peoples to self-determination and the right of small nations to their independence, knowing full well that the break-up of states is no solution at a time when, on the contrary, efforts are being made to group nations together to facilitate development.

The question is not one of suppressing administrative borders, which are tending to become transparent, but to ensure that states respect their minorities: their languages, customs, and cults. At the beginning of the century, Breton was forbidden in France, just as Kurdish is today in Turkey or Iraq. Clearly, tiny territorial divisions are a catch, since nations that are too small cannot survive by themselves, as in the case of the Corsicans or the Palestinians. But this is no reason for not finding a solution to their problems. We proclaim the inviolacy of the arbitrary borders of modern states, which often divide peoples, as in Africa, and, in doing so, we sometimes deliver entire peoples over to the medieval tyranny of kinglets rebaptized as presidents, abandoning defenseless minorities to be deprived of their civil rights and to extermination under totalitarian regimes, as in the case of the Tibetans delivered up to the Chinese.

Primitive civilizations considered the earth as a common asset. The appropriation of certain territories by states or individuals is a debatable right. At the same time, safeguarding the earth and its living species against exploitation or brutal destruction is a duty for all. This is the question that has finally been asked about the Antarctic.

The question as to whether the land belongs to those who make a garden of it, or to those who make it a desert has been raised, often without justification, by the Israelis against the Arabs. In 1848, when the "Americans" took California away from the Mexicans, Marx wrote "Without violence nothing is accomplished in History. Can we say that it is a bad thing that California has been taken away from those lazy Mexicans, who did not know what to do with it?" By a curious turn of the wheel, the Mexicans are now invading a country that has become prosperous.

Should not ecology, which represents the common interest, become the basis for the right of peoples to occupy a territory? Are not the exploiters of Amazonia committing a crime against humanity and against the survival of living species? Are not the industrial civilizations destroying animal and vegetable species, ending up by depriving whole areas of the globe and their peoples of all possibility of survival?

Nowadays, the rapacity of governments and industrial mafias is increasingly bent on destroying the conditions of life in which freedom and the rights of man have a meaning: whoever is aware of his duty easily becomes a victim. In the confusion of ideologies, social classes, human relations, and systems of government—which, according to Hindu theory, is characteristic of the end of the Kali Yuga, in which we are currently living—attempts to define the rights of man without taking his corresponding duties into account are doomed to failure: to a return to the law of the jungle, the law of the strongest, which we call fascism, or of the most numerous, which we term democracy.

Democracy is a social system that can only work where the parties concerned are equally aware of their duties. Despite its tendency, since the fall of communism, to affirm its hegemony and impose its ideology, it is not a universal panacea, and its spread must not serve as a pretext to free us from our obligations.

Notes

Foreword

1. See Jean Canu, *Mille ans d'une famille normande* (Valognes, 1980).

2. Alain Daniélou, *Le Chemin du Labyrinthe*, 2d ed. (Monaco: Éditions du Rocher, 1993).

3. Republished by Flammarion in 1987. See "Other Works by Alain Daniélou."

4. See Alain Daniélou's *The Way to the Labyrinth: Memories of East and West*, Marie-Claire Cournand, trans. (New York: New Directions, 1987).

5. Daniélou, *Le Chemin du Labyrinthe*, 381 [freely translated here from the revised French edition]. See note 4 for a reference to the English edition of this book.

6. Unpublished statement by the author found by Jacques Cloarec in 1998.

7. See the "Other Works by Alain Daniélou" at the end of this volume.

Preface

1. As Daniélou remarks, "Swami Karpatri, whose teachings I faithfully followed, had set up a cultural movement, the Dharma Sangh (association for the defense of moral and religious values), in order to bring about a return to traditional cultural and societal values. He criticized the socialistic ideas put forward by the National Congress of Gandhi and Nehru, as well as those of pseudo-traditionalist reformers such as Aurobindo or Tagore, which claimed to return to an idealized tradition, but which were actually imbued with Western ideas. At the same time, Karpatri was very hostile to the ideas of the Rashtriya Svayam Sevak Sangh (association for the defense of national values), which

advocated methods inspired by Fascism in their struggle against Congress and modernistic ideas. He was not against Vedic orthodoxy, often hidebound, but was very attached to pre-Aryan Tantric Shaivism (Hinduism is a synthesis of these two streams of thought). . . . At no time and in no way did I ever wish to get involved in political movements, either on the one side or the other." See *Le Chemin du Labyrinthe*, 380.

2. Certain terms, such as "race," have clearly undergone a semantic development that makes it difficult to use them nowadays. Should "race" have been replaced by the term "ethnic group" in this book? Regarding this we should keep in mind that Daniélou detested the word "ethnomusicology," in which he saw an implied racism, and that he deals with such questions at length, especially in "The Hindu Caste System," and in his response to the biologist J. Ruffié in "Evolution and Freedom." We must thus let Alain Daniélou take responsibility for his choice of vocabulary, fully persuaded that his work, his life, and his actions, particularly in campaigning for the recognition and respect of all the world's cultures, protect him more than anyone from any accusation of "racism."

3. An intensive and well-documented analysis of the desacralization process in the West can be found in the first chapter of Seyyed Hossein Nasr's *Knowledge and Sacred*, entitled "Knowledge and its Desacralization"(Buffalo, N.Y.: State University of New York Press, 1989).

4. "The extinction of species is part of evolution. Today, however, animal and vegetable species are dying at a rate that is between one thousand and ten thousand times higher than that of natural extinction. We are now at a point where a quarter or half of our actual species may disappear before 2050." (Didier Dubrana "L'évolution c'est aussi l'extinction," presentation of the CD-ROM produced by the Natural History Museum, under UNESCO patronage, *Science et Vie*, no. 969, June 1998.) On the denial of the gravity of the ecological problems caused by modern man, it suffices to open any widely read magazine: "Is the Earth warming up? What's the fuss? For three million years its inhabitants have had to adjust to a planetary thermometer that behaves like a yo-yo." Frédéric Lewino, *Le chaud et le froid des espèces*, 30; "When lower than 1%, the presence of G.M.C. can be deemed accidental, propagated from one field to another or during the transport of produce. Furthermore, such a minute quantity is, for the moment, difficult to detect." Chrystelle Carroy, "O.G.M. Les etiquettes de Bruxelles," *Le Point* no. 1453 (21 July 2000): 26.

5. Teddy Goldsmith, *5000 jours pour sauver la terre* (Paris: Éditions du Chêne, 1991).

6. J. M. G. Le Clézio, *The Mexican Dream: Or, the Interrupted Thought of Amerindian Civilizations* (Chicago: University of Chicago Press, 1993).

7. Roger-Henri Guerrand, "Les clairons de la nostalgie," *L'Histoire* N° 69: 1984.

8. Despite the aggravation of the crisis in our civilization and problems connected with immigration, such questions are caricatured and taken over by political groups. Since 1987, in particular, at a time when the organization *S.O.S. racisme* swapped its discrimination policy for one of integration, the notion of respect for differences smelled of heresy and some of the media did not hesitate to put the ecologists into the same category as neo-nazis. As far as sexual minorities are concerned, far from claiming any real right to be different, their organizations have for some years been carrying on a revolutionary struggle for the standardization of behavior and of individuals.

9. Hippolyte Taine, *The Origins of Contemporary France: The Ancient Regime, the Revolution, the Modern Regime: Selected Chapters,* Classic European Historians (Chicago: University of Chicago Press, 1974; orig. pub. 1880).

10. See *A Critical Dictionary of the French Revolution,* François Furet and Mona Ozouf, eds., Arthur Goldhammer, trans. (Cambridge, Mass.: Harvard University Press, 1989).

11. René Guénon, *The Crisis of the Modern World,* 4th rev. ed. (Ghent, N.Y.: Sophia Perennis et Universalis, 2004; orig. pub. 1927).

12. Gilbert Lely, who established parallels between the Terrorists of 1793 and Nazism in *The Marquis de Sade: A Definitive Biography,* Alec Brown, trans. (London: Grove Press, 1962), speaks of "the confluent leprosy of the dogmas of enslavement." See "Idoménée," *Poésies complètes,* vol. I. (Mercure de France, 1990).

13. On the subject of the *Social Contract,* see the closely reasoned analysis by Hippolyte Taine in *Les Origines de la France contemporaine,* Tome I, coll. Bouquins, 1983. (An English edition of this work is referenced in note 9 but as it only contains selected chapters, it is not certain that the passage referenced here is included.)

14. Alain Daniélou, *A Brief History of India* (Rochester, Vt.: Inner Traditions International, 2003).

15. Guy Sorman, *Genius of India* (New York: Macmillan, 2001).

16. Guy Deleury, *Les Indes florissantes,* coll. Bouquins (Paris: Robert Laffont, 1991), 776.

17. Summed up by two powerful images of missionary literature: widows immolated alive and untouchables dying of thirst on the steps of wells reserved for the cruel Brahmans. Daniélou tackles these questions particularly in "The Hindu Caste System."

18. Is there any need to say that such an assessment is still a question for individuals, groups, or minority research workers? If the scales have fallen from our eyes on the subject of Fascism and Nazism and—with much more difficulty—Stalinism, they still haven't done so for Communism, despite the spectacle of the countries subjected to it, and even less so for "liberalism," supported by the mystiques of "development," "progress," "novelty," and the "reign of quantity."

19. See the essay on "Rights and Duties."

20. Sorman, *Genius of India,* 95.

21. Louis Dumont, *Homo Hierarchicus, essai sur le système des castes* (Paris: Gallimard, 1967); *Homo Aequalis* (Paris: Gallimard, 1981).

22. Sorman, *Genius of India,* 96.

23. Ibid., 97.

24. Alain Daniélou, *Virtue, Success, Pleasure, and Liberation: Traditional India's Social Structures, The Four Aims of the Life in the Tradition of Ancient India* (Rochester, Vt.: Inner Traditions, 1993).

25. A puritanism that, at the same time, is allied to pornographic exhibitions, since the latter is a "selling argument," essential to the puritan advance, which consists of denying that the sexual domain has any power of transcendence and any dignity.

Hinduism and Human Behavior

1. See "The Hindu Caste System."

The Hindu Caste System

1. Jacques Ruffié, *Traité de Vivant* (Paris: Fayard, 1982).

Racism and Castes

1. Jean Bernard, *L'Express,* 25 March 1984.

The Hindu Woman and the Goddess

1. Abstracts from a chapter of *The Myths and Gods of India* (Rochester, Vt.: Inner Traditions, 1991).

The Ahir Caste at Benares

1. *Shilappadikâram, The Ankle Bracelet* by Prince Ilangô Adigal, translated from Tamil by Alain Daniélou (New York: New Directions, 1965).

On the Work of Abbé Dubois

1. Alain Daniélou, *While the Gods Play, Shaiva Oracles and Predictions on the Cycle of History and the Destiny of Mankind*, Barbara Bailey, Michael Baker, and Deborah Lawlor, trans. (Rochester, Vt.: Inner Traditions, 1987).

2. Merchant-Prince Shattan, *Manimekhalai, The Dancer with the Magic Bowl*, Alain Daniélou, trans. (New York: New Directions, 1989).

The Dictatorship of the Pen-Pushers, or Alpha-Bêtise-Me

1. Note by Alain Daniélou, 1991: This text, which does not appear to be directly related to the subject of this book, shows how the mastery of a technique—in this case writing—can be the cause of destruction, hegemony, and colonialism over peoples belonging to the oral tradition. The spread of computers and their databases may, in the modern world, be considered as a revolution of the same kind that led to the spread of Phoenician writing in ancient times. Some observers deem that the fall of the Communist regimes is a consequence of these new methods of communication, and their indispensable application to the domination of the industrial civilization, thus proving—if needed—the force of such a process.

Relations Between the Dravidian and African Negro Cultures

1. Marcel Detienne, *Dionysos mis à mort* (Paris: Gallimard, 1977), 183.

Origin of the Texts

The Caste Institution (*L'institution des castes*)
First edition: intended for *Nouvelles de l'Inde*, 1986.

Hinduism and Human Behavior (*L'hindouisme et le comportement de l'être humain*)
Le Monde, 24 May 1961, under the title *"L'hindouisme propose quatre buts à l'homme."*

The Hindu Caste System; Racism and Castes
Miscellaneous unpublished comments and an article published with the same title in *Racisme, Antiracisme*, Méridiens, Klincksieck, 1986.

The Hindu Woman and the Goddess (*La femme hindoue et la déesse*)
First edition: *Historia*, September 1983.

The Ahir Caste at Benares (*La caste des ahirs de Bénarès*)
Amalgamation of two articles: *"L'institution des castes,"* *Historia*, July 1983, and *"A propos des Ahirs de Bénarès,"* *La Musique dans la vie*, Paris, Tome II, 1967.

On the Work of Abbé Dubois: Customs, Institutions, and Ceremonies of the Peoples of India (*A propos de l'ouvrage de l'Abbé Dubois: Mœurs, Institutions et Cérémonies des peuples de l'inde*)
Postface for *The Work of Abbé Dubois*, Éditions A. M. Métaillé, Paris 1985.

Evolution and Freedom (*L'évolution et la liberté*)
Answer to the biologist Jacques Ruffié, *L'Express*, Readers' Opinions, 31 January 1977.

The Dictatorship of the Pen-Pushers, or *Alpha-Bétise-Me (La dictature des scribes ou l'alpha-bétise-me)*
Unpublished, 1984.

The Castes in Modern India; The West and the Merchant Caste
From: *"L'institution des castes," Historia*, July 1983.

Remarks on Cultural Colonization *(Remarques sur la colonisation culturelle)*
Unpublished, April 1986.

Cultural Genocide in Africa *(Génocide culturel en Afrique)*
Published under the title *"Génocides culturels"* in *The World of Music*, International Music Council, UNESCO, vol. XI, 1969.

Relations Between the Dravidian and African Negro Cultures *(Relations entre les cultures dravidiennes et négro-africaines)*
Unpublished, study requested by M. Pouchpadass for a UNESCO meeting, Dakar, 1978.

Rights and Duties *(Des droits et des devoirs)*
Unpublished, May 1991.

Other Works by Alain Daniélou Dealing with the Caste Institution

A Brief History of India. Kenneth Hurry, trans. Rochester, Vt.: Inner Traditions, 2003.

Le Shiva Svarodaya, Ancien Traité des Présages et Prémonitions d'après le souffle vital. Preface by Jean Varenne. Milano: Arché, 1982.

Le Tour du monde en 1936. Editions Flammarion, 1987.

Manimekhalai, The Dancer with the Magic Bowl by Merchant-Prince Shattan. Translated from the Tamil with the collaboration of T. V. Gopala Iyer and Kenneth Hurry. New York: New Directions, 1989.

Shilappadikâram, The Ankle Bracelet by Prince Ilangô Adigal. Daniélou translated from the Tamil with the collaboration of R. S. Desikan. New York: New Directions, 1965.

Shiva and Dionysus. Kenneth Hurry, trans. London and The Hague: East-West Publications, 1982; reprinted as *Shiva and Dionysus, the Omnipresent Gods of Transcendence and Ecstasy*. Rochester, Vt.: Inner Traditions, 1984; and *Gods of Love and Ecstasy*. Rochester, Vt.: Inner Traditions, 1992.

The Complete Kama Sutra. Rochester, Vt.: Inner Traditions, 1994.

The Game of Dice (modified version of the *Contes Gangétiques*) in *The Fourth Ghost Book*. James Turner, ed. London: Pan Books, Barrie & Rockliff, 1965; also translated as *Fools of God*. Madras, New York: Hanuman Books, 1988.

The Way to the Labyrinth, Memories of East and West. Marie-Claire Cournand, trans. New York: New Directions, 1987.

Virtue, Success, Pleasure, and Liberation: Traditional India's Social Structures, The Four Aims of the Life in the Tradition of Ancient India. Rochester, Vt.: Inner Traditions, 1993.

While the Gods Play, Shaiva Oracles and Predictions on the Cycle of History and the Destiny of Mankind. Barbara Bailey, Michael Baker, and Deborah Lawlor, trans. Rochester, Vt.: Inner Traditions, 1987.

Web site: www.alaindanielou.org.

General Bibliography
Provided by Alain Daniélou

Adigal, Prince Ilangô. *Shilappadikâram*. French translation. Paris, 1961.

Apollodorus of Athens. *Biblioteca*. English translation. London, 1971.

Ayyar, C. V. Narayana. *Origin and Early History of Saivism in South India*. Madras, 1974.

Bannerjee, P. *Early Indian Religion*. Delhi, 1975.

Cotrell, Leonard. *The Bull of Minos*. London, 1953–1971.

Davidson, Basil. *Old Africa Rediscovered*. London, 1964.

Dessigane, R. and P. Z. Pattabiramin. *La Légende de Skanda*. Pondichery, 1967.

Detienne, Marcel. *Dionysos mis à mort*. Paris, 1977.

Eliade, Mircea. *Histoire des croyances et des idées religieuses*. Paris, 1976.

Evola, Julius. *Le Yoga tantrique*. Paris, 1971.

Festugière, A. J. *Études des religions grecque et hellénistique*. Paris, 1972.

Heras, Rev. H. *Studies in Proto-Indo-Mediterranean Culture*. Bombay, 1953. (This much-contested book contains a mass of information on the influence and contacts of the Dravidian civilization.)

Jeanmaire, H. *Dionysos, histoire du culte de Bacchus*. Paris, 1958. (The most important work on Dionysism and its continuation in the Christian and Islamic worlds).

Kandapuranam. In Tamil.

Linga Purana. English translation. Delhi: Motilal Banarsidass, 1973.

Nandimath, S. C. *A Handbook of Virashaivism*. Dharwar, 1942.

Paripatal. In Tamil.

Rawson, Philip. *Primitive Erotic Art*. London, 1973.

Sastri, K. A. Nilakanta. *Murugan. Transactions of the Archaeological Society of South India* 7 (1962–65).

Shiva Purana. English translation. Delhi: Motilal Banarsidass, 1970.

Shiva Samhita. English translation. Delhi: Motilal Banarsidass, 1975.

Tirumurukarruppatai. In Tamil.

Wheeler, Sir Mortimer. *The Indus Civilization*. Cambridge, 1953–1972.

Willetts, R. F. *Cretan Cults and Festivals*. London, 1962.

Index

127